Mothering
Mother

A Daughter's Humorous and Heartbreaking Memoir

"Beautiful, told with humor... and much love."

Booklist

O'Dell, a member of the "sandwich generation"—made up of boomers taking care of both their own children and their elderly parents—portrays the experience of looking after a mother suffering from Alzheimer's and Parkinson's with brutal honesty and refreshing grace. She peppers the memoir with scenes from her past, including meeting her adoptive parents ("The first time I saw Mama, I was four years old") and the death of her father. With three children of her own, O'Dell is torn in multiple directions, trying to be mother, daughter, nurse, cook, caregiver, maid, and more to five needy people. Mama's neediness is unrelenting, and O'Dell is at once bitter and sorry that her mother cannot be who she was. When the inevitable end comes, O'Dell wonders why she longed for the free time she now finds lonely and empty. A beautiful rendering of a difficult but all-too-common situation, told with plenty of humor, a touch of martyrdom, and much love. ■ Mary Frances Wilkens/Booklist

YA: Teen readers will identify with the kids' difficulty dealing with their grandmother and fighting for their mother's attention. MFW.

"I love this book!"

"I loved this book! I not only loved it, I lived it. I laughed, I smiled and shuddered reading this book. Her approach, sense of humor and ability to tell the whole truth will make you love it too. O'Dell has captured the essence of every Baby Boomer's struggle to parent our parents." ■ Judy H. Wright, Author of over 20 books

Mothering Mother

A Daughter's Humorous and Heartbreaking Memoir

Carol D. O'Dell

Carol D. O'Dell

Tell Your Stories

KŪNATI

Mothering Mother

For information, contact Kunati Inc., Book Publishers in both USA and Canada.
In USA: 6901 Bryan Dairy Road, Suite 150, Largo, FL 33777 USA
In Canada: 2600 Skymark Avenue, Building 12, Suite 103, Mississauga, Canada L4W 5B2,
or email to *info@kunati.com*.

FIRST EDITION

Designed by Kam Wai Yu
Persona Corp. | www.personaprinciple.com

ISBN 978-1-60164-003-1   LCCN 2006930184
EAN 9781601640031   BIO026000 Biography & Autobiography/Personal Memoirs

Published by Kunati Inc. (USA) and Kunati Inc. (Canada). Provocative. Bold. Controversial.™

http://www.kunati.com

TM—Kunati and Kunati Trailer are trademarks
owned by Kunati Inc. Persona is a trademark owned by Persona Corp.
All other tradmarks are the property of their respective owners.

Disclaimer: This is a work of non-fiction. All events, characters and situations described in it are real. In some instances the author has taken liberties with chronology in the interest of narrative flow. Kunati Inc. and its directors, employees, distributors, retailers, wholesalers and assigns disclaim any liability or responsibility for the author's words, ideas, criticisms or observations.

For my parents, Willie and Noveline DeVault.

Thank you for giving your home,
your heart and your lives to a little girl
with a fistful of seashells, hoping to belong.

Acknowledgements: My mother always said, "Give honor to whom honor is due." I am blessed. Thank you to my husband, Phillip, for loving me since I was sixteen years old, through everything, and for keeping your promise. To our daughters, Courtney, Christine and Cherish, and my son-in-law Nate for all the patience, laughter and tenderness you so generously give. To all the family, friends, church members, doctors, nurses, hospital staff and care providers who showed my mother and me such kindness. To my birth family and my sister, Rosalie and my brother, Benny who welcomed me with open arms and have shown me that you can love two families. My deepest gratitude to Rosemary Daniell, and for the day you looked up from my manuscript and said, "Darlin', this has to get published!" Your warmth, professionalism and belief in women and all writers is phenomenal. To the gals at Zona Rosa, you listened and encouraged me in my lowest of times. To Paula, you took my words and made them better. To my amazing women friends—Debbie, Cheryl, and Meg—your voices, your hands, and your faithfulness carry me. To the Pinckneyville/Borders Writers' group—I cut my writer's teeth around that table almost ten years ago, and it was your patience with my purple prose that gave me the strength to revise and revise and revise. To the First Coast Writers' Festival, Georgia Writers, the Saint Louis Writers' Guild, the Book Mark, and to my writer buds Ruth, Laura, Linda and Bev. To my agent, Lantz, and to James and Derek and the entire Kunati Publishing staff. Thank you all for giving 150 percent and for believing in me and my story.

The Promise

The first time I saw Mama, I was four years old. I stood on the sidewalk of my grandmother's Daytona Beach boarding house and watched Mama's long legs emerge from the shadows of a shiny black Cadillac and her blue high heels press the pavement. As she stood she kept rising and rising, her bright red hair teased and piled high on top of her head.

Mama looked at me and my sister Rosie and Grandma Stella like we needed her help and she had arrived from Atlanta just in time to rescue us from our pitiful lives. She walked right up to Grandma Stella and shook her hand hard and fast.

"It's nice to meet you, I'm Noveline DeVault."

Grown-ups crowded around us, gawking like it was all some show. I knew this woman had come to get me. I knew this was goodbye to my sister and my Grandma. Mama leaned down and her eyes gestured to my little brown tweed suitcase that Rosie and Grandma helped me pack.

"You can leave that here. I'll buy you all new clothes and toys." Mama sounded so bossy. I set it down on the pavement.

Someone must have told me Mama was coming to get me because I cut my hair the night before. Picked up my bangs in one big fistful and whacked them off, then snipped at bits of the rest. I'm not sure whether I cut my hair to make myself prettier—so they'd like me—or uglier, so they wouldn't. I don't recall feeling one way or the other. Just flat. Mama said I didn't even cry.

Mama was big—five feet eleven and a half, she said, but I swear she was over six feet and just wouldn't admit it. She scared everybody, she was so big. She had giant hands. She called them her piano hands. Mama walked through the house like somebody was chasing her, her long arms swinging, the house jolting with each step. Daddy would grab her in mid-stride and pull her down, smashing the newspaper on his lap.

"Willie, stop that." Mama put up a little fight, and then they'd both laugh and talk real low and soft to each other so I couldn't hear. For them to be so different, they actually got along most of the time. She wasn't the same with him as she was with me, though. She couldn't slap him around. At night, they'd talk and talk and talk, and I'd have to holler out from my bedroom at one o'clock in the morning.

"Some of us have go to school, you know."

Mama was as loud as Daddy was quiet. "You got to be bold for the Lord," she'd shout in her sermons. She was an ordained minister of the Assembly of God churches.

Just my luck to get adopted by a preacher woman.

Mama said God saved her at twenty-two. "God doesn't un-call you once you're called, so I'm going to keep on preaching 'til I collapse or the good Lord Himself comes down and takes over." She'd throw her hands on her hips while everyone laughed and shouted, "Hallelujah!" You'd about jump out of your seat if you weren't expecting it, but I came to expect just about anything from her. She'd stand there, hands on her hips, watching the congregation, smiling, her cheeks like little round apples.

When I was good, Mama used to say it was because I came from good stock, that my birth mother was a college graduate. When I was bad, she'd say it was because my mother was crazy and my daddy was a drunk.

———————————

Daddy retired from General Motors when I turned six. Said he didn't want to miss any of my childhood.

I think he forgot Mama would be there too. He said he'd go crazy if he didn't get to doing something other than fulfilling her every wish, so he started building this garage; his second home, is what he called it. He was down there all the time and I didn't blame him one bit.

They had this whole routine: she fixed breakfast around ten, they ate and then Daddy watched *The Price is Right* until eleven, hollering out the prices like he was right there in the audience. Then he headed down to the garage for some peace and quiet.

Mama thought everybody else lived their lives just waiting to do something for her. She couldn't leave me or Daddy alone.

"Idle hands are the devil's workshop," she said.

Daddy was strong, too; I didn't care if he was old. I liked to put my finger in the crook of his arm in church so he'd tighten up his muscle. Even through his suit, I couldn't get my finger back out.

Daddy was quiet and almost sad, but not quite. I thought of asking him what it was that haunted him, but I didn't.

"Carol, come to the hospital."

I knew from Mama's voice, the exhaustion and the flat lack of hope, that Daddy had had another heart attack. This was his fourth: the one he had when I was thirteen, and two in the three years I had been married. It happened in the middle of the night. He grabbed Mama's hand and clutched so tight she thought her bones would break.

I raced to the hospital, hoping and praying I would make it in time. Being newly married and having two young daughters had left me with little time to sit outside on warm summer nights and talk to him the way I had as a child. I wanted to make up for that lost time. I needed a good, long conversation about the stars, sitting next to Daddy, his legs crossed in the too-small lawn chair, both of us falling quiet, thinking.

Mama and I sat with Daddy in the drab hospital room day after day, waiting for the doctors to decide what to do. We knew we didn't have much longer.

"You've brought so much to your Daddy's life. From the very moment we got you, his face lit up every time he said, 'my little girl.'"

Mama looked so small. Her hair was still mostly red, but it had lost its sheen and most of its height.

"He'd brag to his buddies out at the plant, tell them all the cute things you said. They started kidding him at work, nicknamed him 'Papa.'" She smiled and I let her tell me her stories.

"When we went places and people asked him if you were his granddaughter, he'd grin and say, 'No, my daughter.' They'd marvel and say,

'What a man!'"

I settled in the chair opposite her.

Our eyes locked over Daddy, struggling to breathe. Congestive heart failure filled his lungs with fluid. He lay motionless and sedated between us, covered with a thin sheet and thermal blanket. Mama and I could barely move, each of us taking turns sitting up with him. Sleep deprivation left us washed out and limp.

Mama reminded me that tomorrow, November 4, was my adoption day. I hadn't thought about it, but we celebrated every year like an extra birthday.

"Do you remember that day in the judge's chambers?"

I walked back through that door to the warm wood walls and rows and rows of leather-bound books.

"I dressed you in that little red corduroy jumper you loved so much with your little black patent leather shoes and lacey socks. You could always talk like you were an adult. You walked into the judge's office and looked around like you owned the place. You climbed right into your Daddy's lap and asked the judge if he had any paper and pencils—so that you could draw. You were always drawing."

I remembered. The judge had winked at me.

"'Are you up for the task of raising a child?' he asked Daddy. 'Oh yes, sir,' we told him—by then you had already been with us six months. Nothing could have separated us."

She pulled her sweater back over her bare shoulder.

"The first time you called me Mama, I think I cried." She folded her arms and curled her legs to one side of the chair.

"You had been with us several months and never referred to me in any way whatsoever. I was starting to get a little worried. One day, you were in the breakfast room and I was in the kitchen and I heard this tiny little voice say, 'Mama, can I have another piece of toast?'" She paused. "That was the best day of my life." I watched her turn towards me, take a deep breath and close her eyes.

I realized, perhaps for the first time in a long time, that I loved her.

I turned towards Daddy, the mound of his body under the sheet and thin blanket, and I began to doze, dreaming about the times when he would come home from work and I would hide and wait for him to find me.

"Where's my little sweety-pie? I know she's hiding. Could she be under the table? Behind the couch? In the closet?" He started the game even before he got his coat off.

I giggle, giving myself away, and in my dream I am four.

"Is she in the pantry? Is my little sweety-pie behind the door?"

I opened my eyes and looked at Mama. A loose strand of hair fell from her French twist, her teased front collapsing. I noticed the gray hairs in with the red ones, hanging in her eyes. She let them, too tired to care.

"I don't know why the Lord allows us to be separated from each other in our old age. It seems cruel to spend a whole lifetime together only to be torn apart when we need each other the most. I don't understand." She got up and tucked the blanket under his chin, running her fingers through his hair.

"At least I have the assurance we'll be together again."

I drove home sometime after midnight and kissed my girls' soft cheeks while they slept. My arms ached to scoop them up and rock them on that black, rainy night. I'd caught only snippets of them these past few weeks. I needed to do mommy things—take them to the park and feel my hand on their backs as I pushed them on the swing. I rubbed their chubby fingers until they stirred and left before I woke them.

I stripped down and crawled into bed beside Phillip. He held a pillow in his arms where I was supposed to be. I kissed his back and neck until he woke and turned over, whispering inaudible words as he drew me to him. We made love, silent, with our eyes closed. I drifted off to sleep, only to wake to the telephone.

"This is the nurse on sixth tower. Your father's had another heart attack."

Phillip drove me to the hospital, our girls asleep in their car seats, their heads drooped to one side. I pulled the visor down and looked at their cherub faces in the mirror.

They probably won't even remember their Papa.

The world blurred. Every streetlamp, every lighted billboard zoomed by, and I noticed each one as if important.

I prayed for time.

Daddy sat on the side of the bed; his thin hospital gown did little good to cover this massive man. He glanced at me as I entered, then looked down to the floor. His hands, on his knees, braced his body.

The oxygen cord wrapped over Daddy's ears and into his nostrils, irritating him. He adjusted it again and again. I couldn't believe that after yet another massive heart attack he could still be sitting up.

Phillip stepped in front of me and held my mother in his arms. I knelt in front of Daddy, afraid to touch him and break the immense concentration he needed to control the pain.

"I want ya'll… to promise me one thing," he said with ragged breath. "I want you to promise… me… to be good… and… take care of… each other. Promise."

Part I

"If it's not one thing, it's your mother."

Greeting card

Changes

"Mother, I need to tell you something." I snapped her seat belt snug and stood next to her in the open car door, enjoying the crisp October air. "We have to move to Jacksonville. You know, I told you it was a possibility. Phillip's being transferred to Florida, and we want you to go with us."

"We-ll…" Mother answers, looking out the window.

We all knew she couldn't live alone anymore. Moving out of the state was the easiest way for her not to fight us on the subject. For years she had been hinting about us moving in with her, even though her house was too small for my family of five. She just wanted to be the one in charge.

"Are you sure you want me?" she asks, needing the reassurance.

"Yes, I'm sure. I can't think of leaving you here."

"We-ll…" she says, refusing to look my way.

This is going to be a big change, but there's no other way. She's never lived any place other than Georgia. I reach over and pat her hand.

"Do the girls want me?"

"We all want you. Phillip said he'd build you an apartment that will be attached to our house. You'll have your own space, but you'll be right with us too."

"I want to sleep with *you*, Mama." She's talking like a little kid. "*Waahhh.*"

It's not funny. She calls me "Mama" when she thinks I'm being bossy. I don't want to be her mother. For the last few years I've had to become more assertive. Mother is the queen of assertiveness. At nearly six feet tall, she's domineered me both physically and emotionally since the day she adopted me. I've had to fight to make my own way, and I thank the Lord for giving me an overdose of tenacity and spunk.

It isn't easy to tell my mother what to do. I've spent the last fifteen years since Daddy died watching my mother's slow decline. I had to insist she stop driving, take her credit cards because she'll read the numbers over the phone to any salesman or charity that calls, tell her that she really shouldn't eat two Snickers bars for dinner or let strangers in her house—things I thought she knew. Mother is fifty years older than I am.

She doesn't appreciate taking orders from anyone, let alone her own child. Now, she vacillates between fighting off my advice and soliciting it.

"What will I do will all my knick-knacks? I have to have my pretties." She's trying to sound cute again.

Glass and porcelain figurines, post cards, stamps, dolls and military memorabilia line every shelf, closet, and corner. I have no idea what I'm going to do with all her stuff. Even thinking about it makes me hyperventilate.

"We'll figure out a way." It isn't the time to overwhelm either of us with details. I have six weeks to pack two houses, move two kids, a dog, two cats, a husband, and my mother.

"Can we go to Krystal for lunch? I'm just dying for their chili," she asks, "and I need to go by the shoe shop and Kmart."

I look at my watch, calculating how long all of this will take and wondering if I'll make it home in time to cook dinner.

"What do you need at the shoe shop? We just went there last week." I swear she loves having a chauffeur, and I'm not up to another burger.

"Who's going to pack my house?"

"I am." I'm already feeling a wave of exhaustion. "Hey—you know what I want? A tiramisu."

"What's that?"

"An incredible Italian dessert."

"You know what I want?" She plays along.

"What?"

"A peanut buster parfait."

We sit at Dairy Queen and eat our parfaits. Ever since I can remember, I've had this question lurking along the edges, "Was I wanted? Why did my birth family give me away?" I sit in the booth across from this woman, not my birth mother but my mother all the same, and watch as she scrapes the bottom of the plastic cup. There was never any doubt she wanted me. Daddy either. They longed for a child.

Now it's my turn to reassure.

"We want you to move with us," I say, giving her a wink.

Wanting is the easy part.

Boxed In

Boxes are everywhere. Brown corrugated squares sit stacked in every room like the Legos my kids used to play with. I can barely find a place to step, and I've been unpacking for days. I have put Mother in the room next to ours because I think she'll feel better being as close to me as possible during this transition. Also, I don't want her to walk around trying to find me and trip and fall.

Phillip's putting the last coat of paint on her walls, and we don't have all of the beds set up or furniture in place. Chaos rules.

Moving is nothing new. I remember over twenty years ago, a few months after our first daughter, Courtney, was born, we were moving into another apartment, and I had driven over there to clean it before my husband came with the moving van. I set Courtney down in the living room to let her crawl. She made her way to the center of the empty dining room floor and plopped down on her bottom, sucking non-stop on her pacifier and looking around the cavernous room with its blank walls. She began to cry. If she could have talked, she probably would have told me this wasn't home.

I think Mother would just like to sit down and cry. She can't figure out the layout of the house and says she doesn't want to sleep downstairs. I explain that there isn't a downstairs, but her apartment is on the opposite end of the house from my bedroom. It's so far away that she must feel like it's on a separate floor. She keeps saying she wants to sleep next to me. Not in the next room, but next to me. She walks around touching the walls as if they could collapse on her if she were to let her hands down. She sits in my dining room chair with nothing to do. I've made her breakfast, given her the paper and told her I need to unpack the kitchen, which she can see me do from where she's sitting.

I feel as if I've taken everything from her, which she enjoys announcing to everyone, from the bank teller to the podiatrist. She makes sure to note that she's selling her house, moving in with us, and giving up everything—her church, her friends, and her home. I stand beside her as she regales them with her sob story, wishing I could add what I am giving up—my freedom, my privacy, my mind, and that I'm not doing this to hurt her. I'm trying to help. Instead, I smile and pat her hand, hoping she's receiving the sympathy and attention I can't give.

As I put dishes on shelves, my butterball of a cat, Fat Boy, brushes against Mother's leg. She kicks him. She thinks I don't see her, but I do. I pick the cat up, give him some good scratches behind his ears and put him outside, then get Mother a box to unpack. I place it in front of her, cut the top with a sharp knife, open the lid then take out a wad of newspaper and unwrap the first knick-knack, a small glass clown. I take everything off the dining room table to give her space to place the items. She slowly becomes interested, picking up the next wad and unwrapping a glass shoe. She begins to recognize her belongings. Before long, there's a mountain of paper beside her and two dozen whatnots on the table.

"I'm done. Give me another one."

I've barely put away a few groceries. I get another box, cut the top, and open it for her.

"You need to put these away." She points to the glass objects on the table.

I have no idea where I'm going to put all this stuff. I was just trying to give her something to do. I shift the pieces to the far side of the table and go back to what I was doing—only I can't remember what I was doing.

"Hey, you got any Sprite?" she asks.

"Hold on," I say, looking for the green bottle.

I pour a glass and hand it to her.

"It's too cold."

I take back the glass and remove all but one ice cube.

"You got any straws?"

I look around the room—boxes, newspapers, stacks of plates, grocery bags, and canned goods litter every surface. I'm hot and tired, and it's only ten in the morning.

My middle daughter, Christine, appears in the kitchen, still in her pajamas, her short hair sticking every which way making her look like Peter Pan.

"Hey, Mom, you think you could go to the bank with me later to help me set up my account?" She's looking for the milk, which isn't in the fridge, and the cereal, which isn't on the shelf. I wash out Mother's bowl and hand it to Christine with a plastic spoon and tell her to look around for the milk.

"So, can you take me?" Christine asks, crunching on a handful of dry cereal.

"Where's my straw?" Mother interrupts.

The cat meows at the door to come back in.

"Do I look like I have a straw?" I ask, putting my hands on my hips.

She doesn't say anything, so I go over and muss the top of her hair.

She smiles, but I can tell she wants her straw.

Other Days

On a good day, Mother shuffles around with a fair gait, surprising us all. Parkinson's is like that. The way I understand it, the brain stops producing the dopamine it needs to jolt the tiny charges that connect synapses and allow thought and movement to synergize. So, sometimes Mother can walk pretty well, and other times, she's frozen or jerky. We're grateful for the good days when she explores the house, the furniture and whatnots, as if browsing in a fine department store, acting like she's never seen these items before. I often find her standing in my pantry, hand deep in the Cheeze-Its.

Other days—bad days—I hear her faint call from her apartment at about eight in the morning. I am not Miss Cheerful in the morning and avoid all conversation until at least nine, sometimes ten, not until my two cups of coffee have made a full lap around my bloodstream. I rise from my couch after her third call, lay my journal on the table, sip one last drop of the divine, and allow myself to become her human walker. She claims that canes are useless and walkers are cumbersome and, after her many attempts to get them to do as she commands, she winds up tossing them across the room.

I have agreed to stand beside her, her fingers digging into my wrist as she hovers frozen in her bedroom doorway. Changes from carpet to tile, walls to doorjamb, shut down the delicate firing pistons. And so we stand here, silent, shaking and waiting.

I try to treat her when the Parkinson's flares up as I would a stuttering child, with patience and tenderness. She's broken out in a sweat as she's attempted to walk from the bed to the doorway. I close my eyes, still half dreamy, nestled in thoughts of my own bed. I swoon and remember where I am, still waiting for her to move, my head tilted and rested on the doorframe.

After her medication kicks in, she toodles around her apartment rearranging this and that. She loves to whistle and is quite good at it. I like hearing her whistle because it means she's in a good mood. Sometimes she'll come over to my piano and play. She played in church for years and years. Her repertoire consists of old hymns and a few hits from the forties. Her cascading runs hide the occasional mistake of the damaged pinky finger. When she plays, this serene look comes over her face, and I hope she's imagining she's some place else.

I ask her if she'd like to play me a song, but she says she wants to read the morning paper. I help her to the chair, get out the bowl, put in cereal, slice the banana, and lay out a spoon. I slip the paper out of its green plastic wrapper and lay it on the table then walk back to her nightstand to get her glasses. I stand next to her and hold out her glasses. She tilts her head to the side, indicating that I should put her glasses on for her. I take the arms of the glasses and glide them past her hair and around her ears, then position them on her nose

"When I get me a stove I can cook my own meals," she says, looking up at me.

I haven't found a way to tell her that I don't think it would be a good idea for her to cook. I'm afraid she'll catch herself on fire, or an oven mitt, and burn down the house. I avoid the subject, but she's getting annoyed.

I put a large towel in her lap; milk on a spoon has a way of ending up on her gown. She eats while I unpack. She must wake up lonely because that's when she asks me a myriad of useless questions.

"You're moody in the morning, do you know that?" she asks.

"You think so?" I'm being facetious.

"I'm the same all the time."

You can say that again.

I turn on the TV to a Christian station. She perks up, content with breakfast, paper, and a preacher to listen to. She's anxious to go to church. She asks me several times a day. I tell her we'll find one soon. I'm still trying to find my socks.

Color My World

I've got to strip this wallpaper. The whole kitchen is covered with apples. Not that apples are bad, there are just so many of them. A friend sent me a huge bouquet of sunflowers as a housewarming gift. I put them in a large, two-foot glass vase the girls gave me for Mother's Day last year, and the flowers transform the room. I know I have to paint the walls a Van Gogh yellow and contrast it with *Starry Night* blue. Van Gogh's vivid palette calls to me. Whatever joy eluded him in life, he found in art. Freed of his demons, he found his voice, and for those few hours when brush and man merged, all was right with his world. Maybe that's why I'm drawn to him. He found a way to survive the madness. I paint the walls and hope to find my own voice.

"You gonna leave this color?" Mother says, eating some chocolate-chip cookies I left on the counter.

"Yes, I am."

"We-ll. . ." She turns and walks into her room.

Color must be subjective.

Twelve Steps

I get Mother fed and slide out the back door to head down to the dock. Our new house is on the Nassau River. From the dock I can see a wildlife sanctuary of marsh, river and uninhabitable islands. Water is my element, and this holy land that sits on the edge of sea and sky touches something deep within me. Something in me knows that if I'm going to do more than just get through this, if I'm actually going to thrive, I will need nature to nurture me. I find myself sneaking to the dock throughout the day and allowing the serenity to do its work. Pelicans, egrets, red-tailed hawks and seagulls are my neighbors, as well as a few alligators and the occasional dolphin, though I've not seen either as of yet.

I walk down the twelve steps to our boat dock, turning my back on my other life. One, two, three, I count the steps and think about Alcoholics Anonymous. Steps so real and so gritty that only a person ready to change can submit to the process. Here I am, with my own set of steps.

I can't see my house or my world from this fifteen-foot embankment. All I see behind me are vines and bushes lining the riverbank. For a few moments, nothing else exists.

I think it's important that I make decisions right now, decisions about how I'm going to live with my mother and not die inside. Decisions don't just let things happen and tolerate the results. I decide that when I come to the river, I'm not going to bring my journal, or Bible, or whatever novel I'm reading—not even a self-help book—not any time soon. I want to come empty-handed. I want to be present.

Seagulls trace figure eights above the river, casting their reflection as their wings tip the water. I look at them twice, above and below. A fish leaps—*flash!* My heart leaps. I recognize a glint of silver or some other iridescent color I don't have time to name before he belly flops back into his liquid world.

The muscles in my back relax. I pray to be patient, to have the strength to unpack, be a mom, and a wife, take care of my mother, and make sure everyone gets enough of me, enough care and attention to flourish. Sometimes I imagine I'm a giant milkshake and my family is all sitting around me at some fifties diner. Each of them has a straw and sucks on it, red in the face. They grab the glass and tilt it their way, hitting the side with their palm, snatching it from each other to make sure nothing's left. Mother can be the worst.

Part of me dreads heading up these stairs and back through that door. I want to stay here, bottom glued to graying wood. My eyes strain to see the horizon. I want to go and explore those distant waters. Are the dolphins mating yet? Can I see their shimmering reflections, their wild contortions and wordless lovemaking? I stare at the canoe beside me, and I am tempted, so tempted, to go.

I grab the rail, pick up my foot and will myself to climb the steps.

Wedged

We're all still getting used to one another. I have to get used to waking up and Mother being here, hungry and ready to talk. Her incessant questions and constant need for reassurance scrape against my nerve endings. It's only been two weeks.

"Are you sure ya'll want me here?" she asks several times a day.

"Yes, Mother, I'm sure." I'm on the phone but she keeps talking.

"Well, they sure – don't – act – like it." Her words come out in chops.

I know she's talking about the girls.

"They do." I'm trying to call the telephone repair service, there's terrible static on the line.

"They never want to help."

"The girls help you all the time." I'm defending them, and I don't like it. I don't need to.

"I always have to ask."

"Mother, they're teenagers." The telephone company puts me on hold.

"They never say, 'Hi Nanny, how are you today, is there anything I can do for you?'" she imitates how she thinks they should talk.

I look at her like she's crazy.

"Mother, we all live in the same house! You don't go around saying 'hello, how are you?' to the people you live with."

A recording comes on and I am told a number to push, but I'm so flustered that I don't hear it. I hang up. I'll have to try later.

Mother's still chewing on this; it's not over. I hate being thrust into the middle. It's turning into a constant battle. My girls come back with, "What did I do?" They all might as well be in the car whining, "She touched me."

"Mother, *I* want you, we *all* want you. Relax. You're *here* now, and we're all at *home*. This is *our* home. Please give us time to adjust." I think of my own mother angst. I spent the first half of my life trying to get away from her and the second half trying to get back.

The cat walks by and rubs against her leg. I don't know why that cat insists on cuddling up to the only person in the house who would like to throw it across the river. Mother pushes it away with her foot, gentler this time because she knows I'm watching. She looks disgusted. I try not to laugh.

"Go on now, *scat!*"

Great. Now I have to play referee between her, the kids *and* the pets.

The Game

"Mother? You ready? Your doctor's appointment is in less than an hour. We need to hurry." I call through her dark apartment. I don't know why she has to draw every curtain. Was she always like this?

"Help me with my shoes," Mama's frail voice answers.

I come over and kneel beside her. Her ankles are swollen and there's no indentation, just folds of flaky, swollen skin. I stuff her powdered, stockinged feet into her tan, sensible loafers. A scowl comes across her face. She hates these shoes.

"The worst part about growing old is giving up driving and giving up your high-heeled shoes." I've heard her say it so many times my lips mimic her words.

I stand up and straighten my skirt. I'd much rather stay home and continue to unpack. I need to get my house in order. Besides, I have my own errands. I used to try to combine them, but Mother doesn't like to ride along if the trips are not about her. She fusses if I take too long, but I suspect it's really about me not giving her undivided attention.

"You have to wear a slip, Carol."

"What?"

"A slip. You can borrow one of mine. Look in that third drawer. Your skirt is completely see-through."

I look down at my cotton floral skirt. It looks perfectly fine to me.

"I'm not leaving until you get a slip on—I can see clear up to your crack. You're a Christian."

I don't say anything, just jingle my keys.

"We might run into somebody we know," she adds, "You're almost forty. I would *never* leave my house without a slip."

I keep jingling.

"People can see."

"See what, Mother, my legs? That I've got *two* legs?" I spread my knees and point at the two of them.

She fiddles with her beads and purse.

After a few minutes of stalling, she quietly slides open the drawer and pulls out a flesh-colored, nylon, lace-edged, worn-out elastic, safety-pin-at-the-top slip.

"I'm not going out until you put this on—I just can't. I'm too old." She starts to cry.

Oh great. Here we go with the "I'm too old" crap!

I step into that tired piece of slip.

Mama and her slip: score one.

Carol: zip.

Good thing she doesn't check for a bra.

Down the Aisle

"Are you sure you feel like going into the store today?" I ask Mother.

She fans herself with an envelope that has her grocery and Kmart list scrawled on the back.

"I'm sure I want to pick out my own cold cream." She keeps fanning. "Turn on the air conditioner."

"I haven't started the car yet, hon." I call her sweet nicknames partly because it's a southern thing, and as a way to soften the situation and hopefully get her in a good mood.

"You never get the exact kind I like."

We're back to the cold cream, I guess.

I pull the amber bottle of lavender aromatherapy oil out of the glove compartment and dab a little on the vents. It's supposed to be calming. I have a feeling we're going to need it today.

"I also need stool softeners and hair spray. Oh, and let's get some of those Little Denny pies."

"Debbie." I answer. The smell of lavender fills the car. I take in a deep breath.

"Who's Debbie?"

"It's 'Little Debbie' oatmeal pies."

"I don't want a pie. I want those little brown cookies with the cream in the middle."

"I know, Mother, they're called pies." I grab the amber bottle and cram it under my nose.

I stop the car at the shopping center, get out and go around to her side. I take in a deep breath. Mother's outings are taking longer and longer. I open the door, gently lift her feet off the floorboard, and guide them to the concrete. Her hands are shaking today—it's usually just her left foot. She reaches for the dashboard to steady herself.

"Get me a cart. I walk better with a cart." She stands holding onto my arm, but her feet won't move. I strain and reach for a cart with my foot.

She grabs hold of the plastic-covered handrail and pushes the metal basket. It rolls. I can almost see a light come on inside her. She's going shopping. I place my hand on the end of the shopping cart to help her guide it across the parking lot.

"Slow down," she says, "you're going too fast."

"We need to get across, Mother, we're holding up traffic."

"They can just *wait*."

She shuffles about half a foot and stops. The sun beats down so hard it pushes us to the ground. I know she's got to be hot, but I can't make her move any faster. The furrows in my forehead deepen into ruts; I'm aging as we stand here. I look up to see a white work van with two construction guys staring at us. I give them an embarrassed smile. The driver shifts the van into park. I look the other way as two cars line up, waiting for us to cross. The lady in the first car eats a burger and gives me a nod. The teenager in the second car leans out his window to see what's holding him up, then turns the radio up full blast. Other people walk by in a blur. I run my fingers through my hair and nudge forward.

"Stop pulling the cart," Mother says.

"I'm not."

"You are, too. They can just wait!" She yanks the handle, shuffles, but I don't think anything really moves. "Did you see that fat woman? She ought to be ashamed of herself. I bet she weighs—"

"*Mother!*"

I don't care now, I just want to hurry and get into the air conditioning.

"Jesus is coming, you know that?"

I ignore her.

"*I said Jesus is coming!*" She yells to the cars.

"Where did that come from?" I ask.

"Well, all these people need to know."

"He's gonna come while we're in this parking lot if you don't get a move on!"

She looks at me, startled. We both laugh. We finally make it up the ramp. The van and the other cars whiz past each other. The automatic door opens. A rush of cool air welcomes us into the fluorescent-lit world.

"Let's get a Coke, then you go get the tissues and I'll be in cosmetics." Her face lights up like a little girl's who gets to spend half an hour in the Barbie aisle.

"I'll get the Little Debbies," I answer as she takes off down the aisle.

I have this theory; I've decided Mother is like concentrated orange juice. We all are, really. We start out potent, tart and pure—right off the tree. When we're babies we don't care if you like us or if we're pleasing you. We are uncontaminated, unfiltered, and unadorned, with no knowledge of what we should or should not do. In this concentrated version, we are a wild DNA cocktail of mama and daddy, ancestors and humanity, naked and wordless. Instincts—eating, drinking and bodily functions—drive us. We search for satisfactory ways to please ourselves. We propel toward our uncertain futures with blind self-adoration, and for those first few months, maybe a year or two, we are our life in its most concentrated form.

During the next seven or eight decades we become diluted, filled up with waterous thoughts, language, expectations, and experiences. We gain the ability to somewhat satisfy ourselves in every arena from sex to career. Our other goal is to avoid pain as much as possible. We wail at the slightest bit of emotional, spiritual or physical discomfort. We become bloated, self-aggrandized, and then, when we finally figure out how to make things go our way—most of the time—life takes its final turn, and we begin to deflate.

As our mates leave us, and our friends and family trickle into nursing homes or relatives' homes, we realize that all we've built up is beginning to dissolve. We lose our water and distill, leaving concentrated versions of ourselves, only now we have memories, fears, hates and hurts thrown into the concoction.

Mother is at this final stage during which we all reduce to our own cosmic juice and revert back to some pretty potent pulp. She is no longer interested in betterment, learning or growing. She is tart, almost bitter, and that makes it hard to want to spend time with her. She doesn't seem to have the ability or inclination to be nice. It's all about her now, and it doesn't matter whether I have a hangnail or a tumor; it wouldn't register.

Whatever Mother has accumulated along the way is now strong and unpleasant to those of us who live in a watered-down world. I see the things that remain. She can recall a moment of jealousy or disappointment from forty years ago and gnaw on it for days. Most of the actual events, people, and moments she once held so tightly are now forgotten. I now understand something: we are what we are; the only way we can add to ourselves is by experiencing something powerful enough to alter our belief system. If Mother were naturally trusting, she would continue to trust. But since fear has become so entwined, it's now a part of her concentrated self and must play itself out to the end.

I've barely begun to unpack in the three weeks we've been here because Mother thinks she needs to run errands every day. Now she says her eyeglasses need adjusting. She's constantly sitting on them and flattening them to a mangled mess. No wonder the lenses pop out on a regular basis. I take her to a nearby optician, and we make our way into the storefront office. The windows are tinted against the blinding Florida rays, and a rush of cool air welcomes us. A woman's voice says "hello" but all I can do is squint, trying to see human shapes and waiting for my eyes to readjust. Mother holds on to my elbow and I try to find her a place to sit that looks safer than the stools with rollers on them.

A young couple picks out frames, and a large woman stands in front of a workstation where a lady with a pair of pliers is obviously working on her glasses. She looks up, and I assume she smiles, but I still can't see that much detail. I smile back.

I recognize the larger woman but I can't quite place her. Then I remember. She approached my mother at the church we attended last Sunday and told her she'd like to come by and visit sometime. She has a definite South Georgia accent, which to the discerning ear is different than a North Florida one. She weighs somewhere between three and four hundred pounds.

I immediately cringe, knowing that Mother hasn't ever been one to hold back her comments on other people's looks, and lately, in her new concentrated self, she's getting worse. I can't count the times we have been in public and she's blurted out, *"People are just getting too fat! They're letting themselves go. I would never..."* and I talk louder, change the subject, point to a sales rack, anything to shut her up.

I quickly turn Mother to the left and hope she hasn't seen the woman from church yet.

"Whew-wee!" Mother chimes, drawing out the syllables as if it were a song.

Every head in the place lifts and turns toward us.

I know what's coming next.

"She sure is—"

"Mother, come over here and look at these new frames." I practically shout in an attempt to drown out her next, inevitable word.

"*Fat!*" she adds, impudent as a three-year-old.

Promises, Promises

"I'm so glad I got you." Mother says as I push her chair in at the table. "What would I do if I didn't have you?"

I can tell by her tone she's leading up to something. I set her dinner of beef tips over rice, cut to a fine mush, in front of her and tuck a dishtowel over her house robe. Everyone comes to the table.

"Your cousin has her hands full with my sister. If I didn't have you, I'd be all alone."

I wait for the punch line.

"I know you'd never put me in a nursing home." The girls glance at each other and then me with a what's-going-on-look.

Bingo.

"Those places are nothing but *h e double l holes*." The girls smile at her spelling.

"I was smart. I got you so you could take care of me in my old age."

I've been grilled on the horrors of nursing homes all my life, made to swear never to put her "in one of those places." Daddy never said anything about it one way or the other. He didn't worry about things like that.

It takes a minute to process this. I feel used, as if my entire adoption had been for the sole purpose of being her caretaker. I don't think I can move. I don't know what to do next. I know saying something won't matter.

I put my fork down. I've lost my appetite.

She eats her meal with satisfaction.

Unraveling

I'm having a hard time getting over what Mother said. After all these years, she can still twist the blade. Analytically, I understand. We all say things that sound cruel when we don't quite mean them that way, only I'm not sure that Mother didn't say exactly what she meant.

"From the abundance of the heart, the mouth speaks." That's the scripture she quoted to me when I was a child. Now, I'm realizing *her* abundance. And while it's obvious that Mother has had plans for me all along, I can't help but realize that most of us place certain expectations on our children that even we are unaware of. I'm a parent. I know what it's like to have a few hopes and dreams embodied in the new and improved you. Even though I fight this urge, it's there. Having teenagers, and now one young adult, has broken me in enough to realize they're not about to live my dreams, and that's a good thing. Yet I'm wedged between fury and hurt. It's hard to muster up the energy to fix her meals and deliver them with the same enthusiasm I had just yesterday. I'll get over it, literally climb over it, but for a while I need to sit with this one and let it hurt.

Mother's mind is unraveling. Comments like this one have come loose because she can no longer filter appropriate and inappropriate thoughts. And while she's always enjoyed a good dig, at least she knew to protect our future as mother and daughter, if for no other reason than for her gain. It's not that she hasn't been a selfless, sacrificing mother at times. Motherhood carries years of unacknowledged duty and silent responsibilities.

Meanwhile, my life is topsy-turvy. I'm on a twenty-four hour schedule, vacillating between the roles of wife, mother, daughter, maid, cook, and nurse. I haven't been able to watch even a thirty-minute television program or finish a conversation with my husband, much less anything else, without Mother calling my name and insisting it's an emergency. Even within the confines of raising children, there's a certain amount of freedom and the satisfaction that you're the one who's somewhat in charge, at least for the first ten years. I'm finding that when your parent lives with you, those lines are blurred, if not obliterated.

The term "sandwich generation" is ridiculously inadequate to describe those of us caught between raising our own children and caring for an elderly parent. I've got a better one: the "vice-grip generation."

Some days Mother gets so agitated or bored that she follows me around like a paranoiac, stares at me through delusional eyes, and panics if I turn the corner. I didn't realize I was signing on to be her entertainment committee. Planning out Mother's days on top of everything else I have to do isn't something I bargained for.

I'm afraid my promise may be short-lived. I don't know if I can do this to the end because I don't know what the end will be like. I'm afraid her health will deteriorate to the point where I physically and emotionally can't take care of her. Then what? At least when I was home with my babies, they were soft and cuddly and cooed at me, not snapping at me at every turn. I knew that my time with them was precious and that soon they'd be toddling, talking, and eventually moving on to lives of their own. But this downward, or backward spiral of increasing dependency and mounting care is sucking the air out of me. The mere thought of where this could wind up makes me want to grab my car keys, scribble "sorry" on the hall mirror in lipstick, and head south to Key West, to Jimmy Buffet land, to the edge of this continent, and forget my own name.

I know I will do all that I can. I will go and go and go, but I will not lose my children, my husband, my health or my sanity. I know that. I'm not a martyr. That serves no one. Too many years of therapy, self-help books, and a good dose of selfishness will prevent me from killing myself. I know I will go to the very edge of this chasm and strain to make it across. I'm not doing it for her, or even for my family, but for me. It's something I believe in. Maybe losing one family has made me refuse to give up on the other.

She should never have made me promise when I was just a little kid to such an arbitrary statement. She had no idea what the future would ask of either of us. It would wrench my guts to put her in a home and hear the screams and cries she would undoubtedly wail. I can't imagine the look in her eyes, the betrayal that she'll feel, that I'll feel, if I ever have to do this. I can only pray that God will be merciful to both of us.

Please God—don't let it come to this. I don't want to be put in the position of placing her in a nursing home. I need to keep my promise.

Goldilocks

I took Mother to a Pentecostal church near our home. She doesn't like it. I convinced her to try it for a month but she says the preacher's too loud, and the people aren't friendly enough. We've tried two other places. She said she'd go back to one, but she said it with the enthusiasm of a wet dishrag. We tried the senior citizens group at the local recreation department. She made it there once, and by the time I got her back out the door, she was already fussing, "They're ungodly—playing cards and bingo—I'll have no part of it." The director followed behind us like a puppy saying they had Bible study on Wednesdays. "We'll see," Mother said without turning around.

Why is she doing this? I can't traipse all over town to find the perfect fit. Even if I could, I realize that maybe it's Mother—she's losing her social skills.

Mother's always had friends. I don't know what to do. We took her to our church—she sat there holding her ears like a little kid pitching a fit. I've started calling her Goldilocks—too hot—too cold. I'm not sure there's a "just right."

Getting Our Toes Done

"Where are we going?" Mother asks again as we get into the car. I've already told her twice.

"To get your toes done." I know the word pedicure would need explaining.

I walk Mother into the nail salon and help her up onto the pedicure chair. It's high off the ground and hard to get her into the chair. I have to hoist her with all my strength, then hold her in place with my hip while I lean over and remove her stockings. She's never gotten used to pantyhose and still uses garters—not the kind you get at Victoria's Secret, but homemade elastic bands. A petite Asian woman fills the footbath with hot water and squeezes a few drops that foam the water and fill the air with peppermint.

"You got anything to eat?" Mother asks the woman, who doesn't answer, but smiles with that I-don't-know-what-you're-talking-about kind of smile. I put a quarter in the box by the register and hand Mother a small packet of cookies, then get a Sprite out of the drink machine.

"You got a straw?" Mother asks.

Here we go again with the straw thing.

"No, hon, they don't have any straws."

I think Mother likes the way she's sitting up higher than anyone else in the room, on her throne like royalty. Too bad I can't get her a tiara out of the glove compartment. If anyone ever expected to be waited on, it's my mother. I sit in the chair beside her and slip my feet into the swirling water. I figure I need a pedicure as well.

"My, this is strong." Her eyes tear up after sipping the Sprite. She stares down at the young woman, who takes one of Mother's feet out of the water, and places it on the ledge, then begins to clip her toe nails. An older Asian woman comes over and begins my pedicure. She doesn't seem to speak any English and appears to be the younger girl's mother or grandmother. She looks isolated, her features are stern, her thoughts elsewhere. I guess family issues are about the same everywhere.

The woman barely looks at my legs or me. Her hands work methodically, and I wonder what she's thinking, what it would be like to live with your children in a foreign land, to work on people's hands and feet and have nothing you can say to them—for your words to have no meaning.

"*Mmm.* That feels so good! Can you rub my feet some more?" Mother asks.

The younger woman smiles at Mother but turns to me to interpret Mother's Southern dialect.

"She says it feels good," I say more clearly, smiling at her. She keeps rubbing Mother's feet and legs, her hands moving fast over Mother's calves as if they were feathers stroking columns of glass. She talks to the other woman in their native tongue. She has the same cheekbones and the same delicate hands, her fingers identical to the older woman's. Mother perks up and leans forward, watching them talk.

"What are ya'll sayin'?" Mother smiles in a way that's new and odd; wrinkles begin at her eyes and drape like curtains around her jowls, interfolding with eye creases that intersect and go almost to her ears. It's kind of unsettling.

"What language is that?" Mother interrupts.

They look at her.

"Vietnamese," the young girl answers, her hands never stopping.

"Is that where ya'll are from? *Viet-naaam?*"

My face is on fire with embarrassment.

"Yes." She smiles and straightens her spine.

"Say my name. Say my name in *Viet-naam*. Say *Nah–vah–leen*."

I cringe.

Mother swipes the air, as if she's ordering me to make the woman understand what she wants. I just can't do it. I can't bring myself to this level of degradation. Mother and daughter continue to talk to each other in private. I don't doubt they're saying how strange we are and how they can't wait for us to leave. *I* can't wait for us to leave. I'd like to slide out of this chair and crawl to the parking lot.

Mother still gives them that creepy smile.

"Ya'll kin?"

"Kin?" The woman repeats, looking at me.

"Relatives," I say.

"Oh, yes, this is my mother," she says in a respectful but louder voice.

Her mother hasn't smiled yet. Her hands move in a utilitarian motion over my legs, neither irritating nor enjoyable.

"This is my daughter, Carol." Mother motions my way, "Carol, say your name." She flails her hand at me.

I ignore her and pick up a magazine. I'd like to bury my head in it. The two women continue their work, and I hope Mother will forget the whole thing. She starts again.

"Ya'll live in the back?" she asks, leaning forward even more.

"No, we live off Dunn Ave-nue." The young woman says, her words in starts and stops.

Mother's smile hangs in the air. She has no idea where any place is in this city.

"You know Jesus Christ?"

I want to die now.

They don't say anything.

"You go to *church?*" Mother's voice is raised, demanding a reply. Everyone in the parlor can hear her, and several women turn their heads, their hands plunged into the pink, sudsy, water bowls.

"Oh yes, we Cath-o-lic!" the young woman says. I wonder whether she's making fun of my mother—which would surprise and perhaps tickle me—but then I see her eyes light up, and I realize she thinks this will be common ground.

Mother isn't listening. She sits back without acknowledging her reply, already on a witnessing roll.

"Because if you don't, you'll go to hell," she insists.

The woman smiles, unaware of Mother's intent.

I'm beyond humiliation. This isn't Godly; it's cruel, but because Mother supposedly doesn't know what she's doing, she gets away with it. The woman finishes Mother's toes, and I hope that she understood very little of the conversation. I help Mother down from her throne and hold her steady as we pay and head toward the door. The older woman takes my tip, nods, and quickly heads to the back. The young woman is on Mother's other side, helping me walk her to the car.

"This was absolutely wonderful. You're such a little sweetheart. Are you married? Somebody ought to snatch you right up." Mother presses a dollar, a *whole* dollar, into the woman's hand.

I take Mother from her arm and hand her a ten. I wish I had more.

"I'll be back, darling." Mother turns around and smiles in that animated way of hers.

I'm exhausted. But at least my toes are a great shade of Fire Engine Red.

The Sweet Life

If there's a sin scale ranging from one to ten, with ten being murder, then gluttony is maybe a .05. Overeating isn't exactly lying or coveting your neighbor's wife. Hell, you're not even cursing or taking the Lord's name in vain. In fact, it's not even in the top ten, but it is in the Bible that we're not to be gluttons or drunkards or slanderers or gossipers. Over all, stuffing your face seems pretty harmless compared to some of the major transgressions. Religious people can't smoke, drink, or have affairs without feeling a ton of guilt. This doesn't stop all of them. Believe me, I've witnessed some ferocious church scandals that make Washington DC look like Candy Land.

What Christians can do, with a minimum of guilt, is eat. I remember Mother preaching a revival in Macon, Georgia. It lasted for two weeks and, night after night, we all went out to eat after the service, usually to an all-you-can-eat buffet. About fifteen of us—the preacher, the choir director, a few elders, my mother and my daddy lined up at a long table. One night, a small kitchen fire broke out. The staff quickly got it under control, but we were asked to step outside for just a few minutes while the fire department did a thorough check. Five or ten minutes had passed and Daddy, a big man, pushed through the crowd and went back inside. Just before he got to the door, Mother stopped him.

"Noveline, my steak is getting cold. It's a small fire. I'll be all right."

He went on in and ate his steak.

As far as I know, there was never a scandal about Daddy. He kept his sinning strictly to gluttony.

Mother has always been the one with the sweet tooth. I was about eight when I noticed that some of the titles in our bookshelves had unusual names—*HERSHEY and CADBERRY*. Mother hid Hershey bars from Daddy because she said he had high blood pressure and was overweight. I'm sure he would have eaten the chocolate if he had found it, but both Mother and I knew he had a thing for peanut butter. She had other places to hide goodies as well, like underneath the wrapping paper in cabinets, in her nightstand and in the very back of the pantry behind the Post Toasties.

She has a Snickers stash under her bed now, and I let her think she's keeping that little secret from me.

We all need a few secrets. They give us mystery.

But nothing makes Mother's day like a Klondike Bar. I keep them in a small fridge in her apartment and sometimes she helps herself without my knowing. That used to be okay, but lately, she's been taking advantage of the situation. I walk back to her room this morning and find her covered with melted chocolate—her hands, her face, her house robe, even her toes. She looks like a toddler who's eaten a chocolate dipped cone on a steamy July afternoon. I used to strip my girls down to their diapers, sit them in the middle of a picnic table in the Dairy Queen parking lot and let them have at it, then scoop them up and run into the bathroom for a good rinsing before they touched anything. I can't do that with Mother, but I think about doing the next best thing; letting the dog in—she'd get cleaned right up! One of these days I just might do it. Mother might not find it funny, but the dog and I sure would get a kick out of it.

Mother's not left with many vices anymore, and I'm glad an ice-cream bar makes her happy. If I'm not watchful, she'll eat two and then she won't want her supper, and that peeves me a little. But at ninety, I'm not sure I'll ever eat a balanced meal either. I'll just go straight for the Dove dark chocolates and hope I don't burn in hell. All those flames would melt the chocolate.

One Month In

Time is elastic. Einstein says it's relative. We can't get around the fact that we perceive beginnings, middles and ends; in a sense this is a working definition of time. In one short month, I have experienced one very long month. I've learned to stop romanticizing my adult-daughter role as my mother ages. I would say "dies," but dying isn't the issue. It's the conflicts and complications woven into the very fabric of our relationship that twist and warp with time. I used to imagine that Mother and I would sit by the river and drink iced tea, snap pole beans and talk. Mother doesn't even care that there's a river behind our house.

We're having to figure out how to stand next to one another in the kitchen, how to maneuver past each other in the hall, not just physically but even in our thoughts. No one fits every groove of our psyche, habits, or beliefs, and those knots and bumps rub us raw before we develop calluses. As hard as this is, I'm not in a hurry to get to the dying part. I want to face each day and glean whatever sweetness there may be, to truly be here, open my eyes wide and learn to stand next to her, neither one of us shoved to the side, each with a decent amount of space.

Maybe I'll take up Mother's fascination with straws so I can draw every last drop.

Little Deaths

"When I die..." Mother begins many sentences this way. Her fascination with death is a mix of gothic romance and folklore that many older people, especially southerners, seem to possess. Past generations lived closer to death, and out of that closeness grew stories. Mother talks about death while passing the salt or stirring the cream in her coffee.

I tend to glorify death and even imagine my own or the passing of someone I love in a dramatic scene of sorrow and longing. Death in reality is biological. I witness the little deaths every day, in the shell of a snail and the crunch of a leaf. A sexual climax is referred to in French as a "little death." I could use a "little death" about now.

Death and dying are in my future. But I know I'm afraid of it, of what it will be like. I've never actually seen anyone die. I'm curious, apprehensive and dreading it all at the same time. I don't know if Mother will be here, at home, in the hospital, or somewhere else. I don't know if I'll be at her side or if that matters. I don't know if it will be today, next month, next year, or five years from now. I can't think about all this. The *now* is overwhelming.

Never Ending

The *now* consists of needing to call Mother's neurologist for an appointment and to write him a private letter explaining how things really are, noting the changes I see, the things I can't say in front of her. I need to change her sheets every day due to her incontinence. A permanent mound of sheets, towels, and gowns sits in front of my washer, waiting. I have to pick up the food chunks from under her table before they get ground into the carpet. I need to buy a plastic mat, but I'm afraid she won't be steady on the slick surface because of the Parkinson's, so I mark that off the list and write down carpet cleaner—four cans. Scrubbing the carpet might break up the monotony of laundry.

I need to cut her iron pills in half so she can swallow them, cut her fingernails and toenails so she won't look like one of those Taiwanese dancers, put figs on the grocery list, call the post office for the third time and find out why her mail isn't being delivered. She loves to nag me about this one. I need to apologize to the neighbor for Mother calling the police last night and waking them up. She must have called 9-1-1 at about two in the morning. I woke up to the doorbell and the flashing red lights outside my glass front doors. I let them in and glanced out the door, noticing the neighbors standing in their driveway, looking our way. Now I'll have to assure them that there wasn't some sort of catastrophe. Mother's just elderly and gets scared or bored, or thinks every gas pain is a heart attack, or whatever it is that makes her do this. I guess I better warn them that this will most likely happen again.

Mother likes firemen—it's the uniform. She loves dialing 9-1-1, or *nine-eleven* as she says, like it's some shorthand code for club members.

I need to have a talk with her and ask her not to fuss at the kids. They're beginning to avoid her. I'll notice one of them walking into a room and making a U-turn if she sees Mother sitting at the table because she's forever griping that they really don't want her, that *her* mother would never let her go out of the house dressed like that, or that they need to stay home more and help me.

I tell her it's time for them to be on the go and yes, they do love her and want her here, but do they? Do I? I know she needs to be here, to be safe and cared for, but right now I'm not quite sure what I'm getting out of this, what any of us is getting out of this. All I can think about is this list that goes on and on. Each child comes with its very own to-do list of doctor appointments, schoolbooks to buy, clothes and shoes to purchase, not to mention that I need to just be their mom. I get only so many days, just so many car rides, to listen to their daily frustrations and sing oldies on the radio while we share fries and a Frosty. This is a limited engagement.

Phillip works all day long and deserves to come home to open arms and a smile, not a ratty-haired gripe who doesn't care if there's dinner or not. How am I supposed to suddenly be interesting, attractive, and pleasant? How do I keep this family going?

If time is a series of beginnings, middles, and ends, then where are we? One month in and I'm already worn out.

Yellers

Crash! I hear a bloodcurdling scream, drop the laundry and run back to Mother's room, hitting my elbow on the side of the doorframe.

"Mother? Are you all right?"

"No! I almost fell." She holds onto a chair.

"But you're all right." I try to catch my breath; my elbow throbs and is caught in a locked position. "Don't scream like that."

I force my elbow straight. It hurts. I know it won't do any good to tell her not to yell; she's always been a yeller.

"I can't help it," she says and straightens the tablecloth in a nonchalant way.

My adrenaline bottoms out. I'm drained and turn to go back to my laundry, feeling a little sick to my stomach.

Crash! Another guttural scream.

I wait…

"I'm all right," she says, real quiet.

Good Things

Mother doesn't like this neurologist.

"He's not friendly and warm enough," she says as we walk down the hall to his office.

I hush her, fearing he'll come out of a patient's room at any second.

We sit down in two chairs facing his desk and wait. Mother doesn't like to be kept waiting, and I feel her indignation rising. Some doctors have the knack of flattering their geriatric patients. Mother needs a little extra time and attention if you want to get a decent response. Not that I blame her. I wouldn't like to go to a doctor who made me feel like I was on a conveyer belt.

Dr. Baxt comes in from behind us, saying hello to our backs before Mother can properly acknowledge him. He takes a seat behind his large oak desk covered with papers all the way to the corners. He picks up a manila folder and reads the file without looking up. I hope it's Mother's file, but I have no way of knowing.

He scratches his peppered beard, glancing back and forth, flipping pages, raising and lowering his eyes over the bifocal ridge of his glasses.

Mother doesn't like silence and lets out a noticeable sigh.

I stare at the titles of his books: *Essentials of Neuroanatomy and Neurophysiology, Foundations of Neurophysioloy*, and *An Introduction to Neurophsychology*. My eyes shift to whimsical wire sculptures of doctors that line the shelves. They must have been gifts. He seems more like the abstract glass clock out in the hall; the numbers melting and going backwards like a Salvador Dali painting.

Mother squirms. I'm afraid she'll say something rude or ridiculous given this much opportunity. It wouldn't be the first time. On our last visit to Dr. Baxt, Mother shared her "vision," as she puts it, of Daddy sitting on top of a billboard motioning for her to come up and join him in heaven.

The doctor seemed fascinated, but of course he's studied Freud and Jung and has seen brains from the inside out. I would have been happy to melt into the carpet and lie there between the padding and the floor, stuck between humiliation and frustration. I'm not sure why I feel embarrassment for what my mother says or does, but I do. Control issues, no doubt.

I wish this man would speak.

"Hello, Mrs. DeVault. How are you today?" he says in a loud voice.

Mother startles and grabs her purse.

"I'm hanging in there, playing it cool," Mother answers in her ain't-I-something tone.

"Carol, did your mother tell you I saw her in Kmart? She almost bumped into my cart—I think it was on purpose." He winks at me.

Mother shifts and sits up straighter, enjoying being talked about. She lays her hands on top of her purse, always clutching it in fear of theft, no matter where we are. Her left leg shakes. She slouches again, not able to keep up the façade. I look at her and give her a smile. She's trying so hard, but she looks so tired. The edges of her eyes are red and angry. I need to get her glaucoma levels checked and make sure she doesn't have another infection.

I feel so strong compared to her, so full in this chair.

For years she could out-work me, out-walk me and out-talk me. Now she can't even out-eat me. She'll revert to Ensure and Ritz crackers if I don't watch her. I smile in her direction and pat her hand. Parkinson's is hard. She calls it P. D. and doesn't tell many people she has it. She clings to her pride as a toddler clings to a ratty blanket. Now I wonder what else she has. Reality gets harder and harder to come by. Most of our conversations are about family members no longer here, yet she thinks they are.

She reaches into her purse for index cards filled with questions for the doctor. I wrote these cards this morning at her insistence, so I know what's on them. They're the same questions she asked last time. He gets up, comes around to her chair and reaches for the cards, but she has no intention of handing them over.

"Dr. Baxt, will I ever be able to walk again without help?" she recites, her eyes never leaving the card. He starts to answer but she continues, "I don't use a cane or a walker, you know. I refuse to. What I want to know is, when will I get back my ability to walk without an assistant?"

I'm her assistant. I'm the cane and the walker. I know the answer to this one, but she'll never accept it from me, so I let them play this game while I stare at a photo of a boy, about eight or nine years old, in a baseball uniform. His front teeth are missing and he looks as if he believes he could go pro any day. I wonder if this is the doctor's son and if he's grown now, and if he still plays ball.

"Mrs. DeVault, let me tell you a story…" The doctor goes back to his chair and sits down, then leans back. "My wife and I went to Boston a couple of weeks ago for a conference, and we stayed the weekend to see the city. We walked down by the pier—have you ever been there? It's nice." He rocks back and forth in his chair as if it's an old porch swing.

Mother can't stay with a story this long. I've learned to dice up my conversations the way I do her food—into bite-sized morsels. She smiles at him, but it's a blank smile.

"We held hands as we walked along the pier, and I noticed, Mrs. DeVault—we were the only ones holding hands. Holding hands is a *good thing*," he emphasizes, then pauses, and waits for her to get the point. "You know, you aren't a spring chicken anymore, consider it a blessing to have someone who wants to hold your hand." He nods in my direction, leans forward, places his hands on the desk, and laces his fingers together on top of a stack of papers.

He thinks he got through, and he did—but not to her.

Halls and Walls

Mother goes back to staring down at her note cards, working hard to read words that no longer make sense. I've found pages at home where she's been practicing her alphabet. I'm not sure if she's practicing the letters to make her handwriting clearer, or simply to remember them. When I found them, something in me sank. She's losing language.

She fumbles. She can't get her cards in order. I want to reach over and take them, do it for her, but I'm so tired of taking things from her. God, I'm so tired of this. Each year for I don't know how many years now, I've had to take things away one at a time.

Whether it's the neurologist, cardiologist or podiatrist, we have monthly bouts with some unsuspecting member of the medical community who believes his answers should be good enough. These people of status spend each day exercising their authority to tell others what is right or wrong with them only to have it challenged by a cantankerous old woman who is more than their match. Part of me is glad to see that she still has some *umph* as she calls it.

I shift in my seat, feeling the familiar tightening in my abdomen that I have lived with for so many years, the dreading of what Mother will say or do next. I never know when her prejudices or peculiar religiosities will arise and demand an audience. Dr. Baxt is Jewish, and Mother speaks highly of the Jewish race because "Jesus was a Jew," but it still comes out like a put-down or, at the very least, over-attention.

The other week we were on an elevator and she said that I should let the nice African American man hold the door for us: "After all, they like helping." I thought my head would explode. I apologized profusely, even telling him I was adopted. I don't think he even heard exactly what she said but I was mortified. For years I argued with her, demanded that she understand how malicious and insensitive, not to mention downright wrong, her opinions on matters such as race were. I even won a few rounds, but those long-engrained patterns are deep ruts and no matter what I say, she falls back into them.

"May I see your questions?" He tugs on the cards again.

"I'd rather read them to you if you don't mind. Carol? Are you writing down his answers?" she says, not even looking my way.

I nod, pop my knuckles, and cross my ankles. I stare out the window through the narrow slats of the mini-blinds at the glare bouncing off the cars' windshields.

"Let's go for a walk. I want to see how you're doing." He tries to lift her off the chair by holding both of her hands, but can't. She doesn't have solid footing, one side droops and her foot falters. She begins to slip.

I could have told him that you can't get her up that way, but what do I know? I want to watch him try, let him struggle a bit, see what I go through every day.

"Carol, get my other side." Mother orders, then chuckles to lighten the moment and cover her inabilities.

We walk toward the door and the hall that suddenly seems as long as an airport runway.

"I can get around my own house pretty good but I have to have help at church or at the store."

I note her wording: *my own house.*

He asks me to let go.

"Should you increase my medication? I ache all the time," she says, trying again and again to lift her left leg off the ground. "My knees feel like they're going to give out any second."

She crumples to the side of the wall. I move to help her, but the doctor waves me to the side.

"I don't understand it, I feel sixteen when I'm laying down."

He gives her a smile, watching as she pushes off the wall to gain momentum.

"Walk down the hall and let me watch you from back here," he says, his brow tight in observation.

Her left side seems to curve in, her knee concave, as if someone's about to fold that side of her in two. Her shoulder is tilted downward and so is her left hip. She doesn't move her arms when she walks, they just hang. She's no taller than I am; my mother, once a giant to me in her daunting high heels, is crumpled and shuffling.

"Dr. Baxt, I've noticed a decrease in her mobility in the last six months. She hesitates more often and can't start walking again after she's stopped." I block my mouth with my hand and speak low so Mother can't hear me.

"I am not!" Mother swings around surprisingly fast and glares at me. "I think I'm getting better." She turns back to the doctor. "Do you think we could get that nice physical therapist I had last year? She was the best one I have ever had. The others weren't worth a toot." Her voice is high and fake. She doesn't realize he's not the same doctor we went to in Georgia.

I give up and lean on the receptionist's countertop.

Mother lunges, takes a few steps, and then careens into the wall. I look at Dr. Baxt, trying to get him to understand what I see. It's not just how she walks; it's everything. Can't he do something? Her mind, her whole world is collapsing.

He increases her medication and insists she use the cane, and then sends us on our way with a handful of new prescriptions. That means I get to stop at the drugstore. That means she'll want to go in. There goes another hour.

Does he know how fragile our world is? All his job entails is evaluating her and playing around with dosages—there's not much more he can do. He's a neurologist; he can operate on the most delicate nerve endings and the tiniest of vessels, but in this case, it would do little good. Even with his vast knowledge and experience of medicine, it's me who's left. I'm the one at the end of the hall waiting to take her home.

"When do we come back?" Mother asks as I pivot her backside around to get into the car.

"Six months," I answer between lifting each of her legs off the concrete and onto the mat.

"That's a long time from now." I walk to the other side and get in.

"Turn on the air." I shut my door, start the car and turn on the air.

"Can't see as he does much good." She hits the vents to blow her way, but the air's still hot. "Turn it up." I turn it up. We drive for a while, each of us silent. I guess we were both hoping for more.

"He's not my favorite."

"I know, Mother, I know."

Impressions

My middle daughter, Christine, woke this morning to find my mother skulking around in her room.

"You should have seen her, Mom."

Christine does her imitation of Mother tiptoeing around her bed, lifting up a piece of clothing here and there. Christine's shoulders are hunched and her head is wedged between them, arms bent and her wrists hanging limp.

"Mom, it was so hilarious. She looked like a female Mr. Burns from

The Simpsons. Christine is laughing so hard that she can barely keep up the charade.

"What did she want?" I ask.

"Have you seen a little cane walking around here?" Christine says in Mother's high-pitched Southern twang.

"A what?"

"A little cane, about so-high. You seen one walkin' around here by itself?" Christine's on a roll.

"No, Nanny?' Go back to bed. It's six o'clock in the morning." Christine has my Mother down to an art, and I'm balled up laughing so hard I'm afraid I'll spit my coffee across the room.

"Well, if it happens to be hiding in here, you'll tell me, won't you, hon?"

Christine walks out of the room, shoulders hunched, wrists bent, breaking the act by snickering.

We did impressions of Nanny the rest of the day and laughed until our sides hurt.

One For You

I don't want to go anywhere. I've already taken Mother out once this week, and that's all I can do. But she's insisting she has necessary errands and the only way she can leave this house is with me. It's a dreary November day, rainy with a wet chill that won't let go. I have no desire to leave my couch, much less the house, but I get ready and go back to Mother's apartment to see how she's doing.

She's not ready. She stands in her bare feet, and her blouse is undone, her gray hair hangs in her eyes.

"I've lost my gold watch and it's upset me so much I can't think straight." I button her blouse. She's perspiring and frantic.

"I think somebody stole it. I'm not saying who, but I have my suspicions." She's always accusing somebody of stealing something.

"I lose things all the time," I say, glancing around the room.

"I need to go home," she says. This is the tenth or so time she's said this. What's going on?

"We are home, Sweety. You live with me now, remember?" She just looks at me. I finish buttoning her blouse and go over to move some of the papers, envelopes, picture frames, and beads that clutter her dresser. She's scattered them during her hunt, only making things worse. I can't find her watch. I strip her sheets, look under the bed, on her nightstand, then go ahead and put on clean sheets while I'm at it. Her room smells like old shoes, so I spray with Lysol. I wonder if my bedroom smells this way to others? I make a mental note to spray my room as well.

After half an hour, she manages to get her hat on, and I lean down to help her with her stockings and shoes. I wonder if she really wants to go or somehow thinks she has to. She's always been the kind of person who would put nothing off. She lives for her lists. I have to treat her like a two-year-old, not giving in to her fickle emotions, her present-day likes and dislikes, or moods that change on a whim. When I revert back to letting her be the mother, we both regret it.

"I'm not doing so well since that fall. I could have died," she states.

I don't give her a response, though I'm wondering when she fell. I'm still working at getting this stocking past her misshapen toes. I figure she'll tell me all I need to know and then some.

"I could have pulled that TV over on top of me." I've got one of her stockings on and another one to go.

"It's a wonder I got good sense. My head bounced twice."

I realize she's talking about a fall that happened three months ago, before she moved in with us. "Did you have your button on?"

"What?"

"Your button, the one you can push that calls for help? So if you fall and can't get up, you can push the button and they'll call 9-1-1 for you?" I remind her, but she stares at me as if she's never heard of the thing. I straighten the seam of the hose across her toe.

"No, I don't wear it all the time."

"We're paying thirty bucks a month for you to be safe."

"*I know.*" She sounds like a scolded little kid. I feel bad about the reprimand, but when she's wrong and she wants to get out of it, she does her little girl thing. I hate to admit it, but this one's in my own bag of manipulative tricks, and Phillip hates it.

Despite the lost watch and her distracted mood, Mother insists on going, but she hasn't had breakfast, so I tell her we'll stop at Krispy Kreme. I don't feel like cooking, and feeding her breakfast is at least an hour's undertaking.

We drive to the donut shop.

"I don't want one. You get what you want." She pouts.

I order a coffee and a Sprite and twelve doughnuts, thinking I'll take the rest home to the girls. Mother opens the box and grabs a hot donut. Food, I believe, must be one of those true pleasures in life that outlast many others. I should have eaten only one, but when they're hot, they smush between my fingers. I eat one more and it melts in my mouth like toasted marshmallows from a campfire.

"*Umm,*" Mother grunts. I lean my head back on the headrest and grunt myself.

"Where's my coffee?"

"You said you didn't want any." I hope she'll want her Sprite, but she doesn't. "You can have some of mine."

"*Umm.*" Mother eats her second doughnut. "These are sure good, Carol." She sips my coffee. We sit in the car and polish off half the box. It's so good. I can't remember anything ever being this good.

"I found your watch."

"You did? Where was it?"

"Jammed in the front pocket of your purse."

Names

"I've never seen such a big town! We just keep passing more and more buildings."

"Those are trees, Mother; we're on the highway and there's not a town in sight."

"Sure there are… see? Look at all those people?" She points.

"No, honey, they're trees."

"Turn on your wipers. It's raining." I was just about to do that. "When I get home, I'm calling that Bonnie girl."

"Brenda." She's the preacher's wife from a church we visited.

"I'm taking Bonnie out to eat and get more acquainted. I have got to make me some friends."

Brenda. It's Brenda.

"Pretty soon, all your girls will be grown and it'll be you, me and Phillip," Mother says with the jealous satisfaction of a six-year-old girl who has decided she doesn't want a baby brother after all.

"Cherish is fourteen; hopefully we've got a while."

"It'll be here before you know it. Then it'll be just the three of us." I can tell she's been fantasizing. "Keeping house should be easier for you."

Nice. Now she's moved on to the insults.

"We can go off more."

"Just how long are you planning on living?" I didn't mean it to come out that way. No, I didn't mean it to come out at all.

"Hey, that's not a nice thing to say!" There's playfulness in her response. I can tell she's not really upset.

"Cherish will be around at least four more years; that'll make you ninety-five, ninety-six?" Math is not my forte.

"What will you do then?"

"I'll probably finish college and start teaching." I'll probably have lost my freaking mind.

"What would you want to do that for?"

"I'd like to do something with my life other than cook and clean. You worked all your life. You had a great career." I imagine Mother sitting at the back of my classes and dragging her from room to room. She would enjoy correcting me in front of a crowd.

"It was a ministry, not a career. Besides, I'm not going anywhere 'til the good Lord calls me."

I keep listening for His still, small voice, but all I hear is the *swish, swish* of the windshield wipers.

Lessons

"How am I gonna go to church like this?" Mother asks as she struggles to get into the car after getting her hair done. "I don't want anyone to see me this-a-way. I'll never make friends."

Mother holds onto the car door with one hand and the roof of the car with the other. Even though it's mid-November, it is Florida and the roof is hot. I take her hand so she won't get burned, but she doesn't want my help, she wants to do this by herself. A man passing by sees us and insists on helping. He has no idea how long this could take. He stands next to us for a while, not quite knowing what to do, so I thank him and tell him we're okay. I think he's grateful I let him off the hook.

I lift Mother's leg into the car. It's heavy and awkward.

"See? No man should be doing this for me. I don't know why I always seem to get couples that are willing to take me to church. Why can't some single woman offer to help?"

Mother wants to go to church, and yet it's so hard. She wants somebody to come by and get her. Even if all I have to do is get her ready, that's a battle in and of itself. Then there's the slow walk to the car, and loading her in, and the dozens of thank-yous I feel I have to give these people for their charity. By the time I do all that, I just want to go back to bed. She doesn't even want to go to church with us. Ours isn't lively, she says. She wants to pick the church. Now she wants us to go to her church. If we go to her church, which I could tolerate to some degree since I grew up in it, my kids will balk. What do I do?

It's starting to rain and my suede shoes are already soaked. The auburn-haired hairdresser runs out in the rain to bring me Mother's purse. She helps me finish getting Mother situated even though the lady is getting wet too. She doesn't seem to mind. Some people are easygoing and their grace flows, making everything seem effortless.

Mother teaches everyone patience. It's good though; people need to hold doors longer than they want to, wait for someone to cross the street, or not be in such a hurry in line at the grocery store. Not everyone is lightning fast. Waiting patiently, or impatiently, while my mother struggles, reminds me that during the course of a lifetime I must allow myself to be cared for as well as to be the one giving care. We must allow ourselves to become the object lesson, to let others learn from us. It's part of the deal. We don't always get to finish first.

High Heels

"Want to know the worst part about growing old?" Mother asks as I put her feet into her sensible tan loafers.

"What?" I know the answer to this one.

"Having to give up driving and high heels."

Mother has a shoe rack on the back of her bathroom door. Twenty-two pairs of shoes stand like guards at Buckingham Palace, each pair ready and waiting for a turn to strut their stuff. These aren't the only shoes she has, either; there are more in the closet. But these on the door keep her company by being out in the light where she can see them, run her fingers over the toes whenever she walks by. There are black patent leather shoes, pumps of every hue and tone, alligator and snakeskin, satin evening shoes and gold sandals. All have been around a decade, two decades, or more, all have a story to tell.

Mother still has pretty legs. I tell her, and she smiles and says, "Yes, I do, don't I?" I'm beginning to see this elderly beauty emerge, not that it's emerging for the first time, but that I'm seeing it for the first time. I can appreciate the lace-like veins in her hands and her striking white hair. I no longer see mere old age, but the exquisiteness of time, its delicate wearing down and polishing of a life.

I have to force her to wear these loafers. She despises them, but the podiatrist says they're a must because of her bunions and hammertoes. Her feet are contorted. Vanity, Beauty's less-than-attractive stepsister, extracts her price. Mother's arches sag and the doctor says she's permanently shortened her hamstrings by wearing high heels for so long, and that's why it hurts for her to walk flat-footed, even around the house.

Mother may not get to wear all of her high heels, but she dresses them up on the shoe rack like Barbie dolls. They get shoe buckles—buttons, pins and tiny creatures decorated in rhinestones or beads. Mother has matching purses and color-coordinated scarves. Beads hang over an old tie rack next to the shoes to keep them company. I'd tell her about *Sex and the City* and that this whole shoe fetish thing is alive and well in America, but she detests anything that refers to sex, so I don't bother.

I kneel in front of Mother and try to cram her feet into these ugly shoes. There's something humbling about kneeling. Sometimes I resent it and feel taken advantage of, and other times I'm glad to be asked to get down on my knees, the traditional position for prayer. I gather the stocking in my hands, collecting an inch at a time until they're bunched between my thumb and forefinger. I maneuver the nylons past her toes, with all of their bunions and corns interrupting the way, then glide the stockings up her legs. I've learned to be careful; Parkinson's has made her legs excruciatingly tender. I slide the hose past her swollen arthritic knee, roll them over the garter two, maybe three times, then shove her foot into the powdered shoe.

I came into Mother's room this morning and all of her shoes were on the floor, along with purses, beads and bracelets in a big pile. I asked her what was going on.

"I'm going home with you, aren't I?"

"Mother, you *are* home, you *live* with us." God I'm tired of saying this over and over.

She's more flustered than usual. I wonder what's the matter, if she's gotten into some medication or something.

"I know, but I need to go upstairs, and I thought I might need to pack a few things."

"We have no upstairs, it's just one little ledge—see?" I go over and point to the small step-down ledge, an eighties-built rendition of a sunken living room.

She leans over and gathers two or three mismatched shoes, some beads, and shoves them into an empty purse.

"You don't need to bring your shoes to walk down the hall."

"You don't know what I might need!" she snaps.

"Why did you do this?" I lean over to sort the stack, but I get that head-rush pass-out feeling from my low blood pressure. I'm just throwing shoes or purses to the other side of the mound. More work.

"You don't have to pick up a thing. I'll do it all myself." She lunges toward me but loses her balance. I reach back to steady her and fall on top of the pile. High heels and purse handles jab my hands and hips. I manage to keep her from falling but have no idea how I'm going to get up and hold her up at the same time.

She won't look at me. I don't know what's going on. I get her seated in the recliner and get her a glass of milk. She gulps it down, then burps. I tell her to go lie down and relax, but it doesn't do any good.

Mother's always been in a hurry. When I was little, she would tell me to get out of the way. "I can do it while you're thinking about it," she used to say, and now I'm wondering if that's what I'm saying to her, at least in my actions.

"Why don't you come lie down for a while?" I suggest again, picking up some scarves.

"Don't you pick that up." She's hoarse. I stop and lead her over to the bed. She falls down hard, bouncing as she hits the mattress. I take her neck back in my hand and lay her head on the pillow, then swing her legs around, fluff the pillow and pull up the sheet. She rolls over to face the wall.

I pick up the shoes and all the purses and beads, suspicious and wondering what turn we've taken.

Remote

Mother can't figure out all this "high-falutin' machinery," as she calls it. The phone rings, she answers.

"Hello. Hello? Hello!" She doesn't know she's picked up the remote control.

"Hello!"

No one answers. She sets it on the table, thinking she's hung up the phone, but somehow she's knocked the real phone off the hook. It starts making that noise. I reach over and hang it up.

I look at her but don't say a thing.

"They must have hung up," she says.

I agree. Someone has definitely hung up.

Sweetness

"I could go at anytime," Mother says as she walks into my kitchen and puts one hand on the counter, the other on her hip. "I've got health issues."

I'm getting to know her lines too well. I keep loading the dishwasher, think about taking the roast out of the freezer for tomorrow night's dinner, remind myself to call the dentist, and hope I haven't put it off so long that I have to have a root canal.

"You don't know what it's like not to have a mother around. I couldn't hardly stand it when my mother died." She opens the refrigerator to browse, but stops, her own words hitting her.

"You're right; I don't. I've got you." I realize she needs to hear that I need her. She's showing me that some hurts stay with you.

She doesn't think about my being adopted or that my birth mother died before I could find her—that I have other "Mother issues." I reach past her into the refrigerator, grab a pudding cup and the tub of whipped cream, and gently lead her away from cooling my entire kitchen. I sit her down at the table, pull back the plastic pudding cover lining, and spoon some whipped cream on top.

She begins to eat, lost in her world of jumbled thoughts. She's always been sensitive about her own mother. I've been careful to hear what she does and doesn't say about their relationship in order to figure out what has shaped her and made her the way she is. When I was little, she seemed to idolize her mother and to miss her terribly. Her mother died the year before I was born, and although I was adopted four years later, she was still grieving. Only in the last few years has Mother said anything other than gushing praise about her mother. She told me her mother was "nervous." It was more how she said it that made me curious to see if she'd say any more.

That's when she added that her mother was "critical."

"I could never do anything right. I couldn't wash dishes good enough or cook a roast good enough…" Mother looked like one giant knot when she told me that.

I stood there amazed at what a hold our mothers have on us.

I sit down next to my mother and have a pudding. Extra whipped cream.

Trump Cards and Hope

She's right, most likely. At ninety, almost ninety-one years old, and with Parkinson's and heart disease, Mother will go before me. I need to look at this, although she uses this trump card so often it's hard for me to get in a tizzy over her latest "I could go any minute" routine. She has the strongest will of anyone I know, and I'm of the belief that will has a substantial say-so when it comes to longevity. Still, I feel as if death has moved in with us. He flew in like some nasty housefly when the door was left open too long, contaminating everything in his path.

I know that death is here because I know what it's like to live with hope. When each of my babies was born, the atmosphere around them was holy, fresh and clean. Children, unlike the old, are expected to live, and that expectancy lingers in the air. It took years for this sweet aroma to wear off. I would get a whiff with my goodnight kiss, nestled between the nape of their necks and their damp curls. I'd give in, some ancient part of me remembering my own holiness. By the time they were nine or ten, the scent had begun to fade or was replaced by hormones, but I've never forgotten what it was like.

Mother's not dead, but she's leaning that way. Everyone she loves is "over there." She has more invested in the other side now, and all she needs to accomplish around here is just about done. Life has become a cycle of waking, eating, shuffling about, and trying to engage her mind in something she deems useful, like balancing the checkbook, which she can no longer do, or getting a stain out of a blouse. Even conversations, sermons and

directions, things that once seemed necessary, now cause her to doze off
by their insipid repetitiveness and a nagging suspicion that it all doesn't
matter any more, and I wonder, what is that line we cross? What tells us to
pay attention, that things are important?

She's fallen asleep, her arms folded on the table, cradling her head. I
lift her sleepy shoulders just as I did my babies from their high chairs and
walk her back to bed.

Our Favorite Doc

Both Mother and I look forward to going to Dr. Carlin, her
ophthalmologist. He's a short, zippy kind of guy with a hilarious take on
life and a sharp tongue to go with it. His office staff acts like they enjoy
showing up at work just to see what he'll come up with next.

We go often, every few months, I'd say. Mother lives by the cliché "nip
it in the bud." She should be the poster child for prevention.

They know me so well that last week when they were talking about
the doctor's upcoming birthday party, he turned to me and said, "Hey, you
wanna come? You practically work here."

I used to have a life.

"What would you do if I were your Mother?" Mother asks the doctor
as to whether or not to operate on her eyes for glaucoma.

"Don't ask me that right now. I'm mad at my mother."

I wonder if she'll be moving in with him any time soon.

No Bacon?

I need to go to church. I need to wear a dress and sit on a pew and sing
a hymn and pray. I desperately need to know I'm not just out here on my
own. I dress and hurry to fix Mother some breakfast. I place cereal, toast,
coffee and cut-up bites of cantaloupe in front of her, then hand her the
little silver tray of pills, the same silver tray she always handed to Daddy,

and give her some water to take her medicine with.

You can't hurry Mother anymore. She's worse than a preschooler meandering down the sidewalk, pausing to examine a ladybug on a blade of grass and pocketing every pebble.

"Are you sure I take this purple pill now?" Mother stares at the silver tray as if I'm trying to poison her.

"Yes, Mother."

"Where's the yellow one? I need to take the yellow one." She dumps the pills from the tray into her hand.

"No, Mother, that's with lunch. You take these with breakfast."

"*Is it breakfast time?* I thought it was late afternoon."

"Yes, honey, it's breakfast. Swallow these pills and then you can eat."

"Where are you going?" She looks around the room, tilts her hand, and drops the purple pill onto the floor. I find it on the carpet.

"Church, and I need to hurry." I put the pill on her tongue.

"Is it *Sunday?* I need to go to church, too." The pill drops out.

"No, Mother, you're not strong enough. Phillip is staying home with you today." I pick it back up.

"I can get ready in a hurry."

"Mother, take these pills. I need to go."

"*Aw,* you'd wait for me." She reaches in her pocket and pulls out a long strand of pearls then puts them on over her housecoat. I rub my face to keep from chuckling at her attire or screaming at how long this is taking.

I think of what she's really like, of the Sunday mornings of my childhood and our intricate dance of preparation. The ironing that commenced on Saturday afternoon, the cleaning out of her purse, the polishing of everyone's shoes, the check of the nylon hose for runs, the dab of clear fingernail polish… on and on… late into the night, beginning again early on Sunday morning, culminating in southern perfection. Now, it's a sling of the beads over a well-worn housecoat and she's good to go. This isn't like her.

"No, I can't wait for you, honey. Maybe you can go next Sunday, but you can't make it today." I don't like the sound of my own voice, the hurry inside me.

"Who's gonna stay with me?"

"Phillip. Now take these pills and sit down and eat." Five minutes later, I've scooted her from the bed to the chair and put the tray in front of her. She surveys it, scanning the food as if she's a New York food critic, flicking a cantaloupe chunk onto its side with her fingernails. I turn on the television to a preacher I know she likes and take a step back, sneaking out of the room the way I did when my girls were babies so they wouldn't cry.

"What?" She looks around on her plate. "No bacon?"

Tops Are For Tops

Mother loves Krystal. We've been going there since I was six. I remember the tapping sound my Mary Janes made on the tiny black and white tiles of the Krystal on Piedmont Avenue in Atlanta, Georgia. Mother let me sit at the counter and spin on the stool until I aggravated her so much she grabbed my wrist and dug her nails into my arm. I'd wait a minute then get in one more rotation before giving in for good.

No wonder when, thirty-something years later, I ask her where she'd like to go on our weekly outings, she requests Krystal. She's more than eligible for the senior special of a chili, two Krystal burgers and a small Sprite for two dollars and ten cents, which she fusses is too high a price.

"You see Isley on TV this morning?" she asks, with half a burger in her mouth. I know he's a minister, but I don't want to have a conversation about the man.

"He was telling it just like it is. Jesus is coming."

I reach over and brush off the small piece of steamed bun that hangs on her lip.

"He's not gonna put up with all this wickedness for much longer— young people shackin' up together, doin' all sorts of things. All this talk about Clinton, he ought to be ashamed of himself. Oral sex... if your daddy ever—"

"What do you want at the grocery store?" I try to change the subject. The people behind us have stopped chewing and are listening to Mother's ranting on the evils of oral sex.

"Isley told it like it is. Tops are for tops and bottoms are for bottoms!"

A bite of burger gets stuck in my throat, and I have to cough. The people behind us are snickering.

"You hear me? Tops are for tops!"

"*Mother!*"

"Well? If they can discuss it on the nightly news, I reckon we oughta be able to sit here and tell it like it is. If your daddy ever once tried any of that funny stuff on me—"

"I don't want to hear this, Mother."

She tries to interrupt.

"I am *not* talking to you about..." I can't even say the word in front of her.

"You and Phillip don't—"

"Let's go."

"I'm not done eating."

I stand up. The lady behind us is snorting and pounding her fist on the table. I almost laugh myself and have to cover it with a cough.

"Phillip's never—" she begins again.

"*I don't want to talk about this!*" I head toward the doors without her.

She swings her legs around from underneath the booth. I walk back and help her up.

"I don't know why we can't have a simple conversation."

"I am not talking to you about this." I dump the trash and place her tray onto the ledge. The woman behind us scoots out of her booth and runs to the restroom while the other woman with her heaves in the aisle. I take Mother's hand and help her through the door while she goes on, "Well, you don't have to get all upset."

Demon Dog

"Come here, little puppy." I chase a friend's miniature pinscher into Mother's apartment.

"What's that?" Mother asks.

I pick up the dog. He's wriggly and won't hold still.

"It's my friend's dog. This is as big as it will ever get."

"*You don't say.*" Mother exaggerates, puts her hands to her face. She reaches out like she's about to touch the dog, but stops, laughs and puts her hands back up to her face again.

"What's so funny?"

"I just can't get over it." She leans over, puts both hands on the table and laughs some more. It's good to see.

"He was back here a minute ago, and you know what I thought he was?"

I wait. She wheezes and can't talk for a minute.

"A little demon."

I think of asking when was the last time she actually saw a demon, but I decide not to. I don't really want to know the answer.

Tuesdays

A few years ago, *Tuesdays With Morrie* made the bestseller list. It didn't impress me much.

"Tuesday, my foot," I used to think, "The real story is the wife or the daughter or son—whoever opens the door every Tuesday. *There's* the real story, not the fancy writer who whips in once a week and jots down a few notes. It's the family who lives the story. Ask them what they've learned; they're probably too tired to tell you."

I recently checked the audio book out of the library and listened to it. I have to listen to books instead of reading them now, since my sitting time is non-existent. I swear, Mother has a sensor in her room that beeps every time I get comfortable. I've been reading about dying, trying to garner whatever wisdom and insight has already been penned. I didn't think I'd like *Tuesdays with Morrie*. Sports writers don't sound like very deep people to me.

I realize now I was just being jealous. Jealousy is something I've found that most adults experience regularly but rarely own up to. I was wrong. His writing is good, his metaphors are strong, his humor and personal revelations are honest and soothing.

Mitch Albom may not have been there the other six days of the week, but he was there on Tuesdays. He did what was asked of him. He showed up. The wife, the mother, the son, whoever they were, were probably not writers; that was not their calling. They were not asked to do this task. They opened the front door and allowed the one who was up to it to come in, week after week, pay attention and take notes. Albom, in turn, holds his door open for anyone who cares to spend an afternoon with life, death and all that lies in between.

I have my own door to hold open.

The Mask

Mother has what they call "the Parkinson's mask." Her muscles won't cooperate: they won't move her feet when she wants them to, and they won't hold a pleasant look on her face. She appears to be grumpy or vacant even when she's not. The one time of day I can count on her sour expression to break is at seven p.m. when the *Andy Griffith Show* comes on. I feed her supper then. She doesn't like me to call it dinner because that's what we Southern people have on Sunday afternoons after church.

Mother sits in her recliner and eats off the TV tray. I tuck a hand towel in her housecoat and sit back there with her for a while. We can't eat together every night. It takes her so long to eat that everyone's finished, we've all sat around and talked for a while, then cleared the table, loaded the dishwasher, and I've thrown in a load of laundry—while she's still playing with her peas.

But a few minutes into Andy, especially when Goober Pyle or Barney

Fife comes on, her long wrinkles get drawn into an exaggerated smile, her mouth gapes and even her eyes, usually dull and half-closed, widen in anticipation of the next antic. She moves her still-elegant fingers together to a point under her chin, as if in prayer. She says things like, "They can really get into a mess!" and "He's the dumbest thing you ever saw!" She hisses in silent laughter, her cheeks rosy with the flush of delight.

Perhaps this show brings a distant memory, from forty-odd years ago when she was in her fifties, still young and vibrant, and television was new. It takes her back to a simpler time, with less complicated plots, not so many vixens, or at least not showing it all, and no cursing or killing, just one shenanigan after another. I enjoy watching her more than the television and seeing that mask lose its grip. I'm grateful for Andy.

Taking Sides

The pets love Mother's room. Our beagle, Floppy, never wants to leave, knowing there is an endless supply of crumbs to sustain her. Kismet, my rowdy Alaskan Malamute puppy, follows the three cats, Dunkin, (affectionately known as Fat Boy), Donut and Evi, (short for "inevitable") to the apartment in hopes they'll find the door open so they can have a pet version of a frat party.

Pets don't care if you're old, smelly, or fussy. Pets are one of life's gifts, but Mother can't stand any of them. She says she didn't grow up with animals and just can't get used to them, and she is not about to try. I wish she could; they'd be such wonderful company. Give me a cat and a book and a cup of coffee and come back in a week. Instead, she yells for me to come and get them. I pick Fat Boy up, pet his gray fur, kiss his forehead, and shoo the others out with my foot. She doesn't know what she's missing.

"Here's your breakfast, Mother."

Kismet follows the promise of food and stands next to me. Her Alaskan Malamute tail curls all the way around, touching her back, her tongue hangs out to one side, her ears fold over, giving her a childish countenance.

"That could turn me against you," Mother says, giving me a sour look as she nods toward my puppy.

"Don't make me choose between you and my dog."

Crazyville

"When are we going home?" Mother asks as I help her sit in the recliner next to her bed while I change the sheets.

"We are home, Mother."

"No, we're not."

I pull off the pillowcases, smell the afghan, and decide to wash it too.

"Where's all my things?"

"Look around, there's your dresser, your TV, your clothes."

"I want to go home. Will you walk me across the street to my house?" She has this polite tone in her voice that tells me she doesn't know who I am.

"We *are* home. Don't you remember we moved to Jacksonville over six months ago?" I spray the plastic mattress liner with Lysol, put down a fresh pad for her inevitable accidents, then a clean sheet. I do this every morning.

"Jacksonville?"

"Yes, Mother, Jacksonville." I gather the soiled linens, throw them in the hamper and take them to the washer.

"*Hey, you*, where are we?" she asks as I come back into the room.

"Jacksonville." I answer with my head under the bed looking for cups and trash.

"Oh that's right… where's your daddy?"

"Daddy's in heaven. I think you mean my husband, Phillip. Phillip's at work."

"Oh, yeah, I know that." She crosses one leg over the other, then starts swinging it in a casual manner while she watches me straighten her room.

I empty her trash, but go through it first—there's no telling what I'll find. Last week it was the remote control, a shoe and a coffee mug.

"Where is he?"

"Work." I lift her gown over her head, squeeze out the washcloth, put it in her hand, and then turn away to make up her bed so she can bathe in privacy.

"When did we...?"

"Last year." I go ahead and fill in the blank.

She lets me dress her without a fuss, which is a relief, and I help her get back into the clean bed.

"I just want to go home. Why can't you take me home?"

"You *are* home, Mother! We *all* live under one roof. *You* have a bedroom and *we* have a bedroom. We've been here almost a year." The tension rises in my voice. I push it back down.

"And *this* is my room?"

"Yes, this is your room."

"*You don't say...* She looks around. "Where do we live again?"

I can't help but laugh. It's either that or scream. She laughs too and I lean over and kiss her on the top of her head.

"Crazyville, Mother, we live in Crazyville."

Part II

You are permitted in time of great danger
to walk with the devil until you have crossed the bridge.

Bulgarian Proverb

Going Down

"Nanny, where are you going?" Christine asks as she puts her hand on our front doorknob to block my mother from leaving. I hear all this from the kitchen. I stop slicing the red onions I'm about to add to my salad, listen and decide to let Christine handle it.

"Move. I'm going downstairs."

"We don't have a downstairs, Nanny."

Mother insists we have a downstairs. I've tried over and over to explain that it's just a ledge. We have one upstair and one downstair—no plural.

"Get out of my way, I need to go downstairs and see those people."

"What people, Nanny?"

"The people downstairs!"

There's such desperation in Mother's gruff voice. I lay down my knife and walk softly down the hall. I peek around the corner and watch as Christine slides her body between my mother and the outside world.

"Nanny, let's go sit down," Christine says in an authoritative tone. She'll make a great mom one day.

"Let me ask you this, *Miss Smartie*. If we don't have a downstairs, then how are all the people *down there* gonna get out?"

I wait to hear the answer to this one.

"*Mom!*"

Pete and RePete

Christine and my mother stand toe to toe. Christine's hands are on her hips and she's trying not to lose it. She can see me out of the corner of her eye and I try not to smile and betray us both.

"How long have we been at this store?" Mother turns and asks me. Busted. I've been sucked into it now.

"It's not a store, Mother, we're home. You're in Jacksonville."

"I know that. At least that's *what you tell me*. But let me ask you this— how long have we *been here?*

"About six months."

"Then *where's* all the customers?"

"*There are no customers! We're at home!*" I'm yelling. Why am I yelling?

I don't want to yell. I know I'm only egging her on, and why would I want to do that? Maybe it's PMS. Maybe months of this insanity is finally getting to me. If I have to answer the same redundant question over and over today I think I'll… she's staring at me and I've got to get this situation under control.

"This is our home. You moved here, with us, to Jacksonville, remember?" My words are smooth and even, on purpose.

"We-ll… this is the first I've heard about it." She pushes past me, knocks me against the foyer mirror. I take her elbow and try to guide her toward the family room but she jerks away from me.

"Why didn't ya'll tell me?"

"We did, honey."

"I don't know what to think about you being so secretive…"

I try to help her sit down easily but she throws herself back in the chair and makes a face as if it hurt.

"…though you always were as a child." She looks at me with an angry scowl.

She barely spoke to me for weeks the last time she got this notion into her head. I try to be careful with my words. She stares at me, brings up one arm and puts it on the armrest of the chair, then touches the side of her prominent cheekbones with her long nails in an old-fashioned gesture of elegance. Her wrist is bruised and slightly green from a recent near fall. She's still giving me this awful look.

"Mother, you moved with us last September. This is our home. We built you an apartment, and it's attached to my house next to the kitchen." I give her time to take all of this in.

"We live together." I speak calmly and clearly, thinking my next job should be as a negotiator for jumpers.

"What *I* want to know is… how long have I been *here*…" her hand twirls in the air, as if she could pluck the end of her sentence like a flower and present it to me, "…supervising *you*, at this store?" She smiles but seems perturbed, as if she's ready to fire me. It's all I can do not to laugh or cry or run out of the house shrieking and ripping my hair out in big chunks.

I rub my face and walk back into the kitchen shaking my head.

I have to fix dinner. I need to switch the wash and help Cherish with her math. I take the defrosted chicken breasts and a bottle of Zinfandel from the refrigerator. I uncork it and take a swig from the bottle, then pour half of it on the chicken and take another swig. I have no idea if Zinfandel goes with chicken, but I don't care. I can't do this—I can't talk nonsense all day long and then jump back like Alice, returned suddenly to the real world from Wonderland.

I grab the scissors and walk out the back door, go to my barrels of herbs, and kneel to cut some rosemary and thyme. I stop and sit back, landing hard on the patio bricks. I'm so flustered, I can't even cry. The tears come to the surface but won't spill out. I watch the caterpillars eat my parsley. They're fat, with bright green and black stripes. They'll have it stripped in no time. I watch them chomp away at the delicate stalks and decide to let them. I put the rosemary under my nose; take in a deep breath of its pungent smell. I don't want to go back inside. I look out across the marsh. It's a golden amber shade of wheat that makes me want to find my paints; a slight breeze tinkles my wind chime.

I go back inside, get down a wine glass and fill it to the top, emptying the bottle. I stop. I don't want another problem. Not that one glass would do it, but there's something in me that whispers, be careful.

"*Hey you*—aren't you going to walk me downstairs?" Mother says, looking at me as if I'm a new employee.

I Hear You Knockin'

I wake up sometimes, deep in the night, hearing noises—clangs, bangs, clatters and booms—like a symphony preparing to play: trumpets, flutes, violins, kettle drums, all warming up in disharmony. Then I realize it's just Mother and her midnight ensemble—a broken plate, her playing with the telephone or her incessant banging.

I drag myself out of bed and trudge down the hall, remembering the time when she was in the hospital for an obstructed bowel a few years ago. Mother had decided the nurses weren't coming quickly enough whenever she pushed the call button, so she began to save the forks, knives, and spoons from her food trays to bang on the metal bedrails. I found this out one day when I got off the hospital elevator and heard Mother yelling, "*Hey, you—come here...*"

I turned the corner and saw an innocent passerby, having heard Mother, turn his head and quickly reroute to the other side of the hall. Then I heard an awful racket. By the time I made it to her door, I began to think of an inmates uprising in Sing-Sing or some other maximum-security prison.

"Mother! What are you doing?"

"*They won't come!* What else am I supposed to do?"

I looked at the spoon and knife she held a few inches above the rail. She looked at me looking at her, as if I had walked in on her crime spree.

"Is this an emergency?" I asked.

"Yes, it is. I'm in the hospital and *I need help!*"

Some small country was missing its dictator that day.

Her next major banging incident happened about four years ago when she was visiting over the Christmas holidays. *Visiting*—what a lovely word. I woke up one morning to *Bang, Bang, Bang!* I thought perhaps a construction worker with a hammer had gotten lost and decided to work on our house instead. I stumbled into the kitchen where I saw Mother standing in front of a long row of kitchen cabinets. She couldn't see me from her angle, so I stood and watched. She went down the row, opening each of the cabinets—six on one side, four on another, and then the matching ones below for a total of twenty cabinets. She stood back examining the open shelves and then proceeded to slam each one shut, replicating the banging that had awakened me.

"*Mother!* What are you doing?" She spun around.

This was the woman I had spent the last two weeks catering to—fixing her meals, handing her covers, handing her the remote control and cup after cup of eggnog, all in the midst of the busiest, most stressful month of a woman's already over-demanded life.

She tricked me.

"It's seven o clock in the morning and if you bang one more cabinet, I swear I'll…"

How does one threaten one's own mother? Take away the Little Debbies? Take away the Christian Broadcast Network? Send her to bed an hour early, which in this case would only give her enough energy to start banging cabinets at six o'clock instead of seven?

"You wouldn't get up," she said, acting all innocent.

I'm sure she was a banger in toddlerhood. If her old age is any indication of what kind of child she was, I'm surprised her mother didn't end up in Sing-Sing. Especially if she was the nervous type as Mother said.

All I know is that I'm lying in the dark now, cozied up to Phillip, his leg and arm thrown around me and I'm warm and safe and somewhere I hear it, *bang, bang, bang…*

I lie here, willing myself to go back to sleep, until I can't stand it anymore. I'm fully alert, it's three in the morning, and I'm furious. I find her back in her bed with various objects at hand. Last night it was her cane; sometimes it's the phone, the remote control, a plastic cup, a shoe; and she'll bang the hell out of anything she can find—the nightstand, her potty chair, the bed rail, two cups together, anything that can create noise over and over and over. Sometimes it's a tapping, a rhythmical *tap, tap, tap*, sharp and quick, like a pileated woodpecker. Other times it's a thud.

"*Get me outta here!*" she yells. "*You're in big trouble and you just don't know it!*"

That's what I woke up to this morning.

I find her sitting on the side of her bed, whacking it with her cane. I snatch it out of her hand and toss it across the room.

"*Hey, now*, let's don't cause a scene," Mother says like I'm the jumper.

"It's three in the morning. If you're not sleepy, I'll turn on the TV, but – you – have – got – to – stop – the – banging…" I speak in a calm, clipped manner, but my left eye is twitching. I reach up and hold it shut with my fingers, still feeling the twitch.

"*Why, I didn't know it was that late.* I would *never* want to wake you up. Why *didn't you tell me?*"

She's talking screwy.

"If you'll just take me home, I won't ever let anybody know about this."

I can't think straight.

"Good-night, Mother., I'm going back to bed."

At eight a.m. I wake up foggy and disoriented; I can't quite figure out where I am or why I woke up. Then I hear it—*Bang!*

All Circuits Are Busy

Mother's been playing with the phone. It's more like a toy to her now. She doesn't understand the "talk" and "end" buttons that are standard on portable phones, and she knocks the corded one on the floor, leaving it off the hook for hours. If she does manage to actually make a call, she calls everyone from the mayor to her pastor at three o'clock in the morning, racking up hefty long distance charges.

I hate having to take freedoms from her one by one, in this reverse parenting role I'm stuck in.

I've been unplugging the phone and letting her play with it, but then I have to act dumb when it comes to why she can't get through. It reminds me of playing with my girls when they were little and had pink plastic telephones with bells that chimed when they hit certain numbers.

"It's nine o'clock," Mother says as she sets the phone halfway on the receiver.

I hand her an ice-cream bar, folding back the paper edges while I consider how to phrase my question.

"How do you know it's nine o'clock?"

"Because I called nine-eleven."

"You called nine-one-one?" I correct.

She nods.

"And they told you the time?"

"That's their job."

"No, hon. It's not. Don't call them for that. I'll give you the number for time, but 9-1-1 is for emergencies."

"This is an emergency."

"*No, it's not.* You're tying up the line and people with heart attacks and fires can't get through—those are emergencies."

"*They* need to call the fire department."

I'm livid. How long has this been going on? Can they arrest me for what I'm thinking?

"*Do not call them again!*" I unplug the phone from the wall.

"*Aw,* they don't mind."

"*Yes, they do!* Don't do that anymore!"

"Then how will I know what time it is?"

I walk away before my head splits. That's it. I'm taking the phone.

London Bridge

Phillip and I and the girls are eating pizza and watching a movie. We hear a god-awful scream coming from Mother's apartment. Phillip leaps up, makes it back there before us.

"Mom? You all right?"

"I almost fell. Goodness—I've *never* screamed like that before in my life." She speaks like a Charleston debutante, then brushes her hair back and smoothes it, giving us an embarrassed smile. We go back and sit down.

Christine imitates my mother's words with hilarious accuracy: "I ne-*vah* screamed like that *be-fore in my li-fe!*

Things are definitely falling apart around here.

Caregivers

They call what I do care-giving—giving care, what a sterile term. It makes me want to go pick up supplies at The Care Store. There are books and pamphlets on care-giving; it's a buzzword for this generation. I can answer that perennial question, "So, what do you do?" with "I'm a caregiver."

People nod. It sounds noble, and vague.

Bonding is another word that's always bothered me. Nurses write it on your chart to describe your rapport with your baby. "Mother seems to have a hard time bonding with child." Sounds like glue. Both of these words imply distance and formality, techie lingo for organic, old-fashioned terms such as mother, family and love.

You can hire a caregiver and they can dispense care with your morning pills or your mother can move in with you and you can fuss and fight and figure out how not to kill each other. I'm not sure if I've bonded with Mother, but she's getting plenty of care.

Familiarity

In the year Mother's been with us, she's been in the hospital twice. Once was just a false alarm. Every time she panics, she thinks she's having another heart attack, but this time, I know she's really sick. Not because she's complaining, but because she's not. She's had a bad cold and now it's settled in her chest.

"Hear that little kitten?" Mother asks.

I look at her sitting in a wheelchair as we wait for the doctor to see us, her legs covered with her favorite afghan. She would never consent to sit in a wheelchair if she weren't so weak. I had to convince her it was about to rain and that we needed to get her inside as quickly as possible and that's the only reason she agreed.

"That kitten's purring in my chest again. Hear it?"

She's referring to the rattle her breathing is making.

"That's the cutest little sound." She tries to laugh, then stops, unable to get enough air.

"She might have pneumonia; we need to take some x-rays. We'll have to admit her. She needs a few days of IVs."

This would have to happen a week before Thanksgiving. Hospital stays wear me out, but I know she's not breathing well. I push her down the hall since this doctor's office is adjoined with the hospital. We head toward Admissions, which could take hours. I sign her in and we wait. Mother props her arm up and leans her head on her fist. I get a Diet Coke and sit on the orange vinyl seat next to her, too exhausted even to look at a magazine.

During the last few years, Mother's been in and out of the hospital at least three times a year. I've learned to juggle keeping my family going and being at the hospital. Mother isn't exactly Miss Congeniality and it's a toss-up as to who's going to get riled first: the nurses for having to tolerate Mother's incessant requests and pigheadedness, or me because they've messed up Mother's medications and schedule to the point that she winds up going ballistic. Either that or she swings the other way, stops talking and goes catatonic. It takes me a month to get her back home and situated. Parkinson's patients in general don't do well with environmental changes. New patterns on the floors and walls can cause Mother to freeze, and when you add her sparkling personality to the mix, it becomes a fiasco.

I struggle with what the hospital wants to do and not do. Different medicine, procedures, tests are some of the options modern medicine throws our way. Mother is too childlike to make decisions of this magnitude. Even though I have power of attorney, they catch her in some semi-rational sentence and don't even realize the rest of her thinking is skewed. They take her weak, "I'll do anything you say, doctor," and run with it. By the time they consult with me, their mind is made up. Now they're saying she might have a block in her heart and they want to do a stress test and possibly an angioplasty. I don't think she can handle it, and I know I can't. That could mean months and months of recovery—if she recovers at all. I agree to the stress test and tell them we'll see after that.

She doesn't even know she's in the hospital this time; she thinks she's at her niece's house. How would she be able to comprehend what she's agreeing to? She's being prompted to answer, "Yes, I'll have that done." They look at me like I'm the evil daughter who doesn't want her mother to get well.

We make it up to her room, and I fall into my hospital mode. I've been here so many times. Having two elderly parents gave me plenty of hospital practice. Daddy had heart disease from the time I was twelve, and Mother's been in at least five or six times since Daddy died, for her heart, bowel obstructions—I'm too tired to remember what else. I get out the tissues, place the phone nearby, go get the ice and ask for extra juice, another pillow and two more blankets, the whole rigmarole. I know this place so well. It feels too familiar.

Winners and Losers

I lean down and distract Mother while the nurse tries to put in an IV. Her eyes are fixed on Mother's rolling vein, visible under her parchment skin. Mother is crying; tears stream down her cheeks. Even these screams are recognizable and another reason why I didn't want to come. The nurse keeps jabbing and I keep asking myself, *what for?*

"Just a second more, honey," I say as I hold her other hand, rub her hair, and try to soothe her with words I don't believe.

"This is the sweetest daughter in the world," Mother tells the nurse after the IV is started. The tear streaks are still moist. I hold her to one side as the nurse listens to her breathing, placing the small disc in various locations along her back and ribs.

"We've never had a fight," Mother brags, and I wonder what alter-universe she lives in.

"We've never had a fight *she's lost*," I add, giving Mother a wink, but she's uncomfortable and irritated and can't focus.

The nurse isn't really paying attention, either. She finishes her duties and leaves. I wet a washcloth and wipe Mother's face and hands and give her an extra pillow, adjusting it four or five times to get it just right. She struggles to get comfortable, and I hear that kitten again. I can tell she doesn't feel well. Her face is flushed. I wipe her down with a cloth and pull one of her blankets down to help her cool off then step out, find the waiting room, and call home to tell them it'll be a while.

The One

Mother's back in the hospital; it's only been a few weeks and here we go again. I took her to the doctor's for a re-check and now they're telling me that she has a very low blood count. They did a stool specimen and found that she's losing blood and say she needs to be admitted.

"If I were your mother what would you do?" Mother asks the doctor, after he recommends a colonoscopy—an "uncomfortable" (that's the word they use, I'd go for painful or downright miserable) procedure. They explain that a camera would be inserted through the rectum in order to discover the source of her internal bleeding. I have to tell the doctor she's had this done before. Mother's had intestinal problems for a long, long time.

If I thought they could do anything to fix this problem, I would agree, but we've been here before, and I know this scenario will most likely end with them telling us that she needs major surgery, or that they can't find anything, or can't do anything about what they did find. They'll send Mother on her way in pain, exhausted and disoriented.

We barely get settled when the doctor and his entourage of interns fill the room. He rambles on about the possible benefits, talking more to his followers in starched white lab coats, who are new enough to actually take notes and look desperate.

We—I—decide her heart condition, as indicated by the stress test they did just a few weeks ago, probably wouldn't handle a colonoscopy. It could cause another heart attack, which is worse than the slow bleed she's experiencing. But no one seems to remember we are even here, especially not Mother. A few of the nurses recognize my face, but they simply do what they're told. I feel like I'm in *Twilight Zone* or *Ground Hog Day*, going over the same agonizing situation, caught in some time loop of never ending frustration.

"What about code?" One of the interns asks the doctor.

"She has a living will," I say.

"No, this is different," he says and turns back to face his portable class. "If she were to have a heart attack, here in the hospital, would you want us to perform CPR, shock her back?" The doctor turns again, looking at

Mother for a reply.

Mother's lost.

I answer. "I know she doesn't want a ventilator."

"What's that?" She jumps in and I feel like a fool.

The doctor explains in simple language, but he's talking too fast. She can't keep up.

"Remember Daddy?" I ask, trying to draw her attention to me so she'll understand. "The tube he had in his throat when he couldn't talk?"

We've discussed this many times before when she was alert and not burdened with illness and memory loss. I hate thinking of Daddy that way, the large plastic tube taped to his mouth and cheeks, his eyes shut, the machine forcing each breath for him. She told me after he died she wished she hadn't done that to him. I know I'm not making these decisions for her, although it looks that way now. She told me she didn't want to be ventilated if that was the only way to keep her alive. She told me she wants pain medication, but doesn't want a feeding tube. I know these things.

"She isn't capable of making decisions." I get up from my chair to be taller." I have to go on what we've discussed and decided previously."

The doctor turns to the closest intern behind him. The young woman startles, grabs the pen from her pocket and gets ready to write. "It's a DNI—do not intubate."

"I want ya'll to do what you can. I want to go to heaven, I just don't need a push." Mother says, never losing her humor.

I don't remember what happened next, I just remember sitting there, alone with Mother, wondering if we—if *I*—made the right decision.

Quiet House

Mother's been in the hospital for three days. The first day, I stayed, fought off the doctors, argued with the nurses and begged them to give Mother her Parkinson's medication on the schedule we had going, only to be asked at eight p.m., "What medications is she on?" I knew she hadn't had any all day.

"I wrote all this down. I went over it with the nurses. It should be on her chart." I had already fallen asleep, but threw the cover off and paced as I went over the list yet again.

I went home the next day. I had to. I had to let go and hope they would take good care of her. I knew this crew of nurses best and had already spoken to the one who would take care of Mother for the day and told her I'd be in later. Then I went home and fumigated Mother's room, vacuumed, stripped all the covers, bleached her bathroom and tried to get rid of the slight urine odor that lingers no matter what I do.

Today is Sunday and we went to church this morning, my whole family, together. We haven't been able to do this in a while. We sat on the pew, all of us almost too exhausted to take in much. We went out to lunch and our family energy kicked in. We teased each other and relaxed. I felt guilty, as if I didn't have the right to enjoy it this much, that my hands didn't have enough to do. I dropped everyone at home and went to the hospital. I felt better; even this had been some kind of a break. By five o'clock, Mother was dozing off so I left, longing for my own bed and my own dozing.

I come home to a quiet house. My family has gone to the movies. It feels odd, not walking back to Mother's apartment every five minutes, not fixing meals or giving her meds. I think of my future, when she's gone, how strange it'll seem, and how empty.

The phone rings.

"Her blood count is up, you can come get her," a cheery nurse says.

"What?" I ask, stunned, looking at the clock. It's six o'clock at night. Why would she come home now?

"You can come and get her."

I can't think of what to say.

I hang up and cry. Phillip and the girls come home from the movies and ask me why I'm so upset. Christine rubs my neck and shoulders while I cry. I can't seem to stop. I take another bath, dress and cry some more. Phillip holds me, I cave into his chest. He offers to go and get Mother, but there are so many things no one can do but me. I'm so tired. I didn't even know how tired I was until the nurse said, "Come and get her," and it all rebounded on me.

I get to the hospital at 7:30. It's already dark outside. It seems absurd to be dismissing Mother now. I get to her room, pack her bag. Mother just lies in her bed not saying a word. I don't think she even knows where she is. The aide wheels Mother downstairs and I walk beside them in a stupor. We're no better off than three days ago. Her blood count may be up, but everything else is off kilter. They fixed one thing but undid a hundred others.

"This is a mighty big house they built," Mother says to the aide as we get into the elevator.

Mother nods off in the car only to wake up frantic that I'm running off the road. Then she goes back to her comments about how tall the buildings are. They're trees.

Sometime after two, I crawl into bed, too tired to cry anymore.

Shirley

The good part about this hospital stay is that Mother qualified for some sort of aid and we get a physical therapist and a bather to come to the house several times a week. They also delivered a hospital bed. Mother doesn't like it. All this is a mixed blessing. I'm not up for company, and even the act of opening my front door can seem monumental. But Shirley comes and bathes Mother three times a week and I don't mind at all. She's an African American southern woman with a smile wider than her hips.

I've liked Shirley from the first time I talked to her on the phone. Even the sound of her voice makes my shoulder and neck muscles relax. I'm soothed by her languid tone as she calls my mother "sugar" and nestles her nose in Mother's neck after she bathes her. She tells Mother she smells good. Mother doesn't show any reaction at all. I'm so afraid Mother's old prejudices will surface and she'll say something condescending. But I can't tell; her face is back to the mask. The hospital stay has undone all the work I've spent months on—trying to get her to relax, feel at home, trust us, and enjoy life, as well as maintaining a decent schedule of medicine and food to keep her as mobile and alert as possible. It's taken Shirley three weeks just to get Mother to look at her and acknowledge her presence. She can almost get a smile out of her now. She coaxes Mother along by telling her how pretty she is, the way a mother coaxes a fussy toddler.

Mother sits on the potty chair while Shirley bathes her. Mother's skin is so white it could be a sheet out on the line; her tired breasts splay across her stomach, and her soft white hair covers her eyes. There's something serene about Shirley's methodic swish of the washcloth, the squeeze of excess water, and the gentle swipe against Mother's tissue-thin skin. Mother slumps in silence, and yet a calm envelops the room.

I despised the other bathers—their rough wipe, their hurry, their avoidance. No one is more aware of Mother's nakedness, her vulnerability, than I am. I feel as protective of her as I did of my infants. I won't let the bathers in her room without my presence. I want to protect Mother, make sure no one is too familiar, or too hurtful. I'm not sure it's worth my worry and the time I spend supervising could just as well be spent bathing her myself, but Shirley is different. When Shirley comes in, I feel lighter.

The first day Shirley came, Mother had made quite a mess in her potty chair and all over herself. She had never done this before this last hospital stay. I tried to hold Shirley back, making excuses, asking her not to go to Mother's apartment until I could finish cleaning up, but she shooed me away.

"Oh please, girl—I need to see it anyway."

The bedroom reeked. I sprayed Lysol with a fury. Shirley went on about her business while I apologized profusely and continued to spray. Mother coughed and told me to stop.

"We all think our shit don't stink," Shirley said out of the corner of her mouth, leaning over so only I would hear. We laughed.

When Shirley asks how I am, she expects me to tell her. She knows because her mother was given three months to live and lived nine years. I hate stories like that. I asked Shirley how would I know if it was just too much and I couldn't do it.

"Oh, you'll know. Rather, your family will know. You'll begin to say and do things you've never done before."

That scares me.

Shirley changes the sheets and puts some powder on them. She brushes Mother's hair and puts it up in ways I hadn't thought of. Shirley goes about her work with peace, her hands doing the unmentionables with the grace of an angel.

"Come and look at her bottom," she told me the other day.

I didn't want to; she's my mother. But I acted nursey and did.

"See? Her little lady is red. The hospital didn't give you any ointment?"

I shook my head no and went to look for something that might work, laughing at the differences in language.

"Little lady." What a nice way to put it.

Shirley and I spend a few minutes after each session together. I enjoy her company, which is quite a compliment since lately most people irritate me. Shirley watches a little bit of the Food Channel, we exchange recipes, talk about decorating. Girl talk. I miss my friends. Most of them are in Georgia. I haven't gotten out to meet anyone, although there are several nurses at Mother's doctor's offices who seem quite friendly. That's the extent of my social circle.

I gave Shirley a jar of homemade pickles I canned myself after being inspired by a segment on Martha Stewart. I leave the TV on, flipping between the home decorating shows and old movies for company. Shirley said she ate all the pickles by the time she got home. She said she ate them with her fingers; the jar nestled between her knees.

Dread

"Ca — rol?"

God, I hate my name.

I let her call it for a good ten minutes. This isn't an emergency. I've already checked on her a few minutes ago and it's only six in the morning. She had me up half the night. Literally. I got up at two o'clock, then three, four-thirty and six. I finally lay on the couch so I could get to her before she could wake everyone else up. I hear her shuffle into the kitchen and sit at the dining room table, staring at me, waking me up every few minutes with some wild tale that makes no sense. She begins to slap her legs repeatedly.

"What are you doing?"

"I'm freezing. They're like ice."

I lie there. It's not cold in this room and my entire body feels like it's made of concrete blocks. I'm fed up with her. There was no good reason for me to have to get up with her that much last night. She's not sick, she was just wide awake and decided to bang a few things, scream that she was falling, turn the TV on full blast, go into my kitchen and leave the refrigerator door open so long it started to beep. I've seen two-year-olds pull the same stunt.

I fall asleep to a distant whapping and wake up at seven-thirty. She's managed to pull the tablecloth off the table and onto her lap. Eight little blue candle bases are stacked on the edge of the table resembling the Leaning Tower of Pisa. I lie on the couch, still feeling that block on my chest.

I look over at her, trying to figure out what the hell she's got on. It's her fur coat and hat, legs bare, except for the tablecloth and Phillip's house shoes. She loves to take Phillip's house shoes. Her pocketbook is open and there's a banana, a stapler and a small New Testament sticking out of it.

I drink my coffee while she stares at me. At this point I'm just being stubborn. I wish I could wake up perky at seven on the dot and do my morning chores like Snow White caring for her beloved dwarves, but I can't. I wish I could be better. No I don't. Not this morning.

The caffeine rejuvenates what neurons didn't get connected because of my interrupted sleep. I get her pills, give her the banana that's in her purse with a glass of milk, and tell her I'll fix breakfast in a little while.

An Uninvited Guest

"Good morning, Mother. How are you?" I try to be pleasant.

"I'm not saying," Mother answers, rubbing her eyes like a sleepy baby.

"Why not?"

"I don't want the devil to hear me."

Content

My friend Meg came down from Georgia and helped me plaster my kitchen walls. We drank pots of coffee and took turns plastering, feeding Mother and doing dishes, turning my walls from an epidemic of apples to Tuscan-sun yellow. My friend Debbie comes down and cuts Mother's hair, washes it and puts extra conditioner on it then twirls it into a French twist. It's a big job. Mother is like a cat or a witch and doesn't enjoy getting wet. It's so good to have someone here. I've been too overwhelmed to realize how empty I feel.

Each of my friends gives me something when they care for my Mother. Mothers, grandmothers, aunts and older women friends give continuity and community. I need more than the continuity that is my mother and my daughters. My friends come and stay in my house, sleep in my beds, cook meals with me, side by side. They throw clothes in the wash, watch videos, sit by the river with me under the water oaks and Spanish moss, and we complain about husbands, kids, wrinkles, sagging middles, and the thousands of little and big things that scare us.

Losing Me and the One Year Mark

I have to get the oil changed. Mother came home from the hospital almost six weeks ago, and I've barely gotten out of the house except for a quick trip to the store while she's asleep. Errands are piling up.

I call ahead and tell the mechanic to slate me in for 10:30. Even with Mother changed, fed and medicated, I can't leave her too long with only Cherish in the house. It's more than a fifteen-year-old needs to handle. Mother's had it in for her lately. "Why is she so *mean* to me?" Mother whines.

Accusing Cherish of being mean is ridiculous. The child is known for her sweetness and ease. I think Cherish has pulled back because she's getting scared of my mother and her unpredictability. Cherish is backing off and I can't blame her. I mainly just want her to watch out for Mother's safety. I worry about her falling again, but she falls when I'm standing right beside her, and when I'm asleep in the next room, so waiting and worrying are useless.

I dash out the door, hit with a crisp November day. It's clear and bright and there's a chill in the air. I go back in and grab my blue-jean jacket. I drive through my neighborhood and notice a guy out for a stroll with two dogs, each pulling its leash in different directions. A group of women in polar fleece jackets push strollers and walk as fast as they talk. The leaves are cascading down on a stiff breeze. We don't have an actual fall season; the trees seem to lose their leaves at various times between November and April but today, a gust of golden leaves twirls to the ground. It looks as if it's snowing gold. I clip past house after house, my eyes taking in every change. Further on, cars pull into McDonald's and there's a long line at the drive-in teller at the bank. I feel on fire, noticing everything in sharp contrast. It's been so long since I've been out and had a clear mind that everything pricks my senses.

I've lost something this last year. I've shrunk. I get out less and less and I've forgotten how bustling the world is. When I see workmen in vans, telephone installers on the side of the road, or children with their moms in SUVs, I realize that as my mother's life dwindles, she's taking me with her. I'm fighting a slow sadness.

I can't just suddenly get a job and come home at six each night and say, "Isn't it great, everybody? I've found myself!" I've made the decision to be a wife, a mother, and now, my mother's mother. My independence, spontaneity and maneuverability must defer to choice. This too is a season, I tell myself. It won't last forever.

Potential

I've enrolled in college. Am I crazy? Why would I do this now? How do I think I can pull this off? I just know that if I don't keep moving forward that something in me will die. I married at eighteen, attended seminary but never got close to graduating. Now, of all times, I have this urgency to do something more. I've found a school where I can go to classes two nights a week in an accelerated adult program. Phillip says he'll do it with me. He never went to college either. He says he didn't really even think it was an option, being the eighth child.

I used to tell him I married potential. He's done so well in the computer field and we've had a great life—a life we made together. This isn't just about making more money or having a framed diploma. We're ready for more. The girls agree to watch my mother, but I'm not sure they can handle it all, though I'm not giving them credit here. I think I'd pay to have someone come in for those few hours. I just know that I've got to keep moving forward.

"*We-ll*," Mother gives me her usual response when I tell her. "If you did everything you need to do around here, you wouldn't have time for college."

That might be what she said, but I can tell she's proud.

Stamps

"Where are your mom's nitro-glycerin patches?" Phillip calls on the cell phone and asks. I'm with Cherish at her swim meet. The roar of parents cheering and the splashing of water drown out the cell phone conversation. I walk to a nearby picnic table away from the noise to hear a little better.

"Can you hear me? I forgot to put one on her this morning—they're in her medicine basket." I shout into the phone.

"I already looked there. I can't find them and she's freaking out.

"Check in the kitchen cabinet where I keep our medicine and then call me back." I walk around the crowd, looking for Cherish. I don't want to miss her race. The phone rings again.

"I can't find them and she's tearing the place apart—what do you want me to do?"

"Damn! I want to see my daughter swim." I try to think of where they might be. "Can you come up here and cheer her on? This is county finals, it's big, and one of us has to be here. Maybe I can make it back in time."

We pass each other on the road.

"Mother?" I call out as I enter the kitchen; I hear banging before I reach her room. The drawers are pulled out and papers and panties are everywhere. She's kicked all the covers off the bed and she's sitting on the plastic mattress cover, panting.

"What have you got all over you?" I look closer.

White paper patches and colored paper dots cover her face, arms, and chest. I pull one off, trying to figure out what they are. They're stamps. She's taken stamps, torn-up pieces of labels and scotch tape strips, and stuck them all over her face, neck, chest and arms.

"Don't worry," she gasps. "I found them."

"I'd say you have. You've got enough postage on you to go to Australia."

Wanderings

Crash! I roll over; the soft red numbers on the clock read 5:02. I fumble for my robe. In the summer, there's already a soft light to the sky, but it's December and the dark cold goes through me. Mother stands in her apartment living room wearing a thin nightgown, not the one I put on her. She's trembling. The carpet is covered with shards of broken glass. I can't tell where they came from. I don't want to turn on the lights. I don't want to see.

As my eyes adjust to the soft fluorescent glow of the laundry room light, I can tell she's knocked over a set of shelves filled with carnival glass vases, bowls, glass baskets, figurines and pictures. The large statue of Mary that sat in a corner is on its side in three chunks. The head is off by itself; a broken arm and torso inches away from my feet. The base remains next to the wall and reveals a gaping hole where the body broke off.

"You've broken your things."

"They're *my* things to break!"

"But I *really* loved Mary." The hurt slips out. I kneel down and pick up the head. I had taken the statue of Mary into my bedroom when we first moved here. I knew Mother's apartment was so crowded that it might get broken. Mother found it when she was still spry enough to roam the house and demanded it back. I've tried so hard to let her hold on to her dignity that I've sacrificed more than was necessary. I don't want to treat her like she's in a nursing home or a hospital. Her belongings, all crammed into this tiny apartment have made her feel at home rather than displaced. But if anything is going to be left, I'll have to take it out and put it away.

I brush broken glass into a pile off to the side and place a cover on top to keep her from stepping on it. I pick up the larger chunks, thinking I might be able to glue them back together.

"Let's get you back into bed."

I help Mother back to bed. She's unsteady and I'm afraid she'll take me down with her. Her Parkinson's is worse at night after the medication has worn off, yet it has a way of coming and going. Just an hour ago she obviously got out of bed, walked into this room and threw down a shelf. Now she's the statue.

I can't stand the thought of sweeping these objects into the dustpan. Some of these figurines have been in my life since I was four and now they're gone. I have to wait until morning to see if there's anything I can salvage. Each morning I wake to the chaos of her nighttime wanderings. That's when I have to face it.

We haven't moved more than an inch in the last few minutes.

I'm used to this, but at five in the morning, it's hard to take. I pull on her to get going.

"*Don't! I'm gonna fall!*" Her body tightens. I realize she hasn't let go of the railing behind her.

"You've got to let go of the rail, Mother." I hold the one of her hands in mine and reach around back for the other.

"Mother, let go, grab onto my hands."

Her fingers won't budge. Another minute passes. I try to pry them off the rail, but she's got it tight. They won't move.

I understand—the broken shards, the nighttime devastations, the unwillingness and even inability to let go. I get it. I'm being asked to pry Mother loose from this world. She can't do it, or she won't. She's stuck.

Jelly Envy

I sneak into the kitchen and quietly switch on the coffee pot then wait to pour myself a cup, taking care not to rattle so much as the spoon. I carefully and silently open the fridge for cream. If I can just have one cup before it all starts, I'll be grateful.

Mother must lie in bed waiting, listening for the slightest noise, because if she hears me, more times than not she'll call my name, and off we go. If I'm lucky, I get to sit down and catch a few minutes of some morning TV show. Willard Scott comes on with his radio-announcer voice stating some elderly person's name while the Smucker's company sponsor show their photos inside a gingham jelly-jar border.

I hate them. I hate them all. All of these old geezers are one hundred years old—or more. All of them "live at home, drive their own cars, teach Sunday school, and eat bacon every morning of their entire lives, and all, thank the good Lord for great health," Willard informs me with his cheerful smile and shiny bald head.

Yeah, right. Those pictures are over fifteen or twenty years old and I don't buy for a minute that they all drive. At least I hope not because I've seen a few senior citizens who would make a drunken teenager on a drag strip seem like a great insurance deal. And yeah, they all live at home—while they suck the life out of the family who's taking care of them. I'm bitter before the coffee kicks in.

These centenarians remind me of how long mother could live. She'll be one hundred in 2011. I'll be dead in 2011. There's no way I'll make it ten more years like this. Maybe I'll run away, buy a fishing pole, and go live in the Keys. If I'm going to be homeless, it's going to be in the warmest place I can get to and with some way to feed myself. Since Spanish is practically the official language of south Florida, no one will understand my angry mutterings when I tell them, "My mother's one hundred and still living and I've run away from home." I'll be the grubby-looking fifty-year-old with Smucker's strawberry jam smeared on my chin.

A Temporary State

Sometime after Mother's last hospital visit, all of her jewelry came up missing. I'm pretty sure I didn't take it to the hospital with us, but I have no way of knowing for sure. Two of those times she was taken by ambulance with me scrambling to shove a few things in a bag and meet her there. The coin purse she kept her jewelry in is gone. It's not in her purse or drawers, or anywhere. But I don't think anyone took her jewelry.

Mother's nightly raids leave her apartment in shambles. She tears her tissue box to shreds, the tissues and paperboard crammed between the pages of a Bible. Banana peels will be wrapped in underwear, shoes stuck in pockets of coats and brushes and combs turn up in the freezer. I think she's done something with the jewelry, something so bizarre that it might take me months or years to find it, if ever.

I try not to appear obvious as I look through her apartment, not wanting to arouse her suspicions because she could become more paranoid. I told the nurses I'd be calling the police, to report the missing jewelry. But days go by. I look under the chair, and the bed, and move books around, but I haven't done a full-scale search. Am I avoiding the search because I don't think I deserve the jewelry, or do I just need it to stay lost?

Lost is a temporary state. Most lost people and lost things eventually turn up. Lost is not as permanent as gone. In my clouded mind, I think I'm too deadened to face that I've lost something truly valuable to me. I planned on giving each of the girls a piece of the jewelry so each would have an heirloom from her Nanny. I can't face this hurt. It's not the money, though they were quite valuable. My attempt to allow Mother to have her own space with her own things has proved disastrous. The possessions have lost their meanings for her, and lost has become gone, like the parts of our relationship that are gone—times I'll never get back.

Re-gifts

Mother's eccentricity comes to the forefront at Christmas. She's the queen of the re-wrap. We never threw out any wrapping paper when I was growing up. No matter how crinkled, ripped, or layered with tape along the edges, Mother snatched it out of Daddy's hands and mine, pressed it on her lap, folded it then placed it in the linen closet among stacks and stacks of other hand-pressed, pitiful looking wrapping paper. I didn't care how the gifts looked that we exchanged among the three of us, but it did prove embarrassing when we gave gifts to others. I even tried ironing the wrapping paper under a damp washcloth to make it look new, but I know there were a few relatives who noticed.

Mother's actual wrapping skills rivaled her hoarding of paper. For her to have been such a neat freak, she wrapped like a blind spastic. It did, however, go hand in hand with the actual gifts she gave. After seeing Chevy Chase's Christmas movie where the aunt or grandmother wraps up the cat and tries to give it away, I suspect those writers have hidden cameras in my house for inspiration. Either that, or this habit is some psychiatric oddity that falls in the obsessive-compulsive disorder chapter in psychology textbooks.

Mother would always pick things up from around the house to give— a re-gift is what I call it—like some candle or decorative soaps someone had previously given her. She keeps a stash of recycled gifts next to the wrapping paper in the closet. If a gift didn't come from her stash, it had to come from her favorite place, The Last Chance Thrift Store. The name says it all. Everyone wants a dingy glass flower vase you would normally get free with a bouquet, marked twenty-five cents on the bottom with a grease pencil which you can never get off. If you were special, Mother would give you a housecoat with bits of candy wrapper still in the pocket, or a wall plaque with a wonderful country theme of painted roosters and barns faded from too many sunny days in the Last Chance bins. If she really liked you, you'd get her all-time *pièce de résistance*—a smelly old afghan. An afghan is special only if you know the person who made it. If you don't, it's just a lumpy ball of knotted yarn in some hideous multi-colored design that will match nothing in your house. What a lovely gift to wrap in used wrapping paper.

You would think all of this would make me an excellent wrapper, but no. Maybe it's genetic: wait that's not right—I'm adopted. Is this a nature versus nurture issue? Thank goodness for gift bags. You can reuse them and no one notices. And I hate to admit it, but I too have a few re-gifts stashed in the hall closet.

Collecting

It's Christmas day and I wheel Mother to the dining room for dinner. Phillip and the girls are already sitting down and everyone smiles at Mother and makes over her. She's been out of the hospital maybe three weeks and she's still weak. I don't know if she'll stay in this wheelchair, and I think it hits us all pretty hard. She doesn't need it every day, all day long, but some days I need her to be in it.

She hates the thing and acts embarrassed, I can tell by her demeanor. Phillip gets up and takes the wheelchair from me, slides it under the table, adjusts her afghan and asks her if she's comfortable in that wonderful man voice of his. I make her a plate of turkey, dressing, mashed potatoes and gravy, green bean casserole and pumpkin pie. Typical fare, I leave off anything fancy. Neither her teeth, what's left of them, nor her stomach can tolerate anything they haven't had before. She eats her pie first, loaded with whipped cream. She closes her eyes partly due to her eye condition, but I think it's more of a convenient way for her to be here but not be here. I also believe she closes her eyes to enjoy the gift of taste without interruption and to remember Christmases where she was the cook and this was her table.

We gather around the tree to open presents with Mother's wheelchair turned so she can enjoy the festivities, but she doesn't participate much. Every few minutes we hand her another present—chocolate, panties, socks, house shoes, a lap cover, a book about history (which she used to love) and more candy. Nothing interests her but the candy, and she's pried each box open and eaten at least one piece.

In the past, Mother gave the girls presents; she chose an odd menagerie of thrift store items, a few re-gifts, maybe a new bottle of perfume and some cash. This year, I wrote out checks for her and she hands one to each of them. She receives their hugs and holds onto their hands, her lips quivering, her body longing for touch.

Mother's always been odd. Three years ago, Mother gave Courtney, then sixteen, a baby doll bought at the thrift store. The doll's dress stuck out in front at an odd angle, its eyes stuck open with that doll-frozen look. Courtney thanked her, took the toy, which she had definitely outgrown, and lifted the dress to see why it protruded in such an odd manner. On the lower abdomen of the doll, near her private area, were four magic markers that oddly resembled an erection. It was so peculiar that we broke out laughing and couldn't stop. We passed it around the room, each one of us taking a peek. Mother started laughing, too, though she didn't know why. We laughed so long and hard, we all had to pee, which seemed somehow to go along with the doll joke. To this day, we tease Courtney about buying her another doll. Maybe she can start a collection.

That Christmas seems long past. Mother is ready to go back to her room. Her little gathering of candy, handkerchiefs, panties and book are in her lap. I take one picture of her and the girls before rolling her back to her room, wondering if this will be our last photo.

Captured

Cherish waits until Mother's gone to bed to give me her gift. She's the artist of my girls and I know it's a framed drawing by the feel of the box. I rip the paper and see the face of my mother. It's from a photograph I took of Mother and Shirley, her bather. Shirley's hand is holding Mother's face, and Mother's eyes are lifted but reveal a lost state. It is both sad and poignant and captures this time in ways words have no power to portray.

I gasp, and tears flow. Cherish got it. She captured my mother—her beauty, her loss, even the wave of her hair. Even our love for her is somehow held in place by pencil and memory.

Christmas Crazies

It's between Christmas and New Year's and I feed Mother breakfast at our dining room table, pushing her wheelchair under the lace tablecloth. The Christmas candles and flower arrangement still sit on the table. I take the ornaments and lights off the Christmas tree and lay them on the tablecloth, while Mother eats her oatmeal, toast and coffee at the other end of the table. Her eyes are nearly closed as her hand methodically goes from the bowl to her mouth.

She reaches over and picks up a blue glass ornament. I watch as she tilts it to her lips and tries to drink from it. I stop and wait. She sets it back down, takes another bite of toast and then does it again, turning the ball up as if it's a juice cup; her head tilts back and she swallows.

I think of stopping her, but I've learned not to. Sometimes I'm curious as to how far something will go. Is she faking? Is this somehow entertaining her, or meant to entertain me? She seems content to drink from the ornament and I begin to wonder, "Could there be anything in there? Water maybe?"

That's what happens when you live with someone who's hovering above reality. New possibilities arise and you say, "Why not?" I shake the glass ball, just in case, then clear her plate and ask if she wants any more. She says no, so I head to the sink with the dishes.

"Wait, wash this too," she says, holding out the ornament. I take it and pack it away when she's not looking. Ornaments don't do well in the dishwasher.

Double Take

"Where's Carol?" Mother asks sitting at the dining room table after dinner.

"I'm right here, Mother." I call from the kitchen as I feed the dogs.

"No, not *you*—the *other* Carol."

"Well, I'm the only one there is." This is new. I'm used to her not knowing other people, but until now, I was in the safe zone.

"*Hey—you! Come here*," Mother whispers to Phillip, who is in the living room watching the nightly news. He goes over to my mom. She's smiling so he smiles back.

"Where's your wife?" she whispers, with that eerie grin of hers.

"She's over there, Mom. Carol's right there."

"Not that *one*." She shakes her head side to side, curls her finger, and motions for him to come closer.

"That one's fussy. I want the other one." He looks at me and lifts his brow.

I'm waiting to hear what he says to this one.

"You know—I always did want two of you." He winks.

"I don't want her. I want the other one. I want *my little girl!*" Mother's voice is strained.

Phillip puts his hand on hers.

"It's okay Mom, we're right here."

I dry my hands and come over.

"Mother, I'm here. I'm all you've got. I'm the only Carol there is." I kneel in front of her so she can see my face.

"I know that, I just want to know where my little girl is."

"Mom, she's my wife now." Phillip says. "This is Carol. She's the little girl you adopted, she's just all grown up."

"*Shh!*"she interrupts him. He leans in close.

"Who's that old man over there?"

"Where? What old man?" He turns around, "Mom, there's no man in the house but me."

"*Shhh*! See that man? Over there in the corner with the straw hat…"

The night goes on with Phillip trying to find the old man, not knowing whether to play along just to give her something to do, to ignore it, which would mean ignoring her, or try to gently lure her to reality. The old man turns out to be a stack of books in the corner of the living room.

Mother can't seem to understand that "little girl" of hers isn't here anymore. She keeps trying to find the other me. It's odd when someone has split you into convenient portions, preferring one you to another, and yet, don't we all see our loved ones the way we want to see them? Are we not all fragmented? The child me, the one she knows, or knew, is more to her liking.

I take her back to her room and get her ready for bed.

"I'll bring you back some milk, okay?"

"Just tell Carol to bring it in." Tears puddle in the corner of her eyes.

"What's wrong?"

"I just wish that *other* Carol was as spiritual as you are."

Who's My Mother?

"This may be a silly question but can I ask you—who is your mother?" Mother's voice is high and false. She looks up at me, wondering, her brown eyes more alert than they've been since her last hospital stay. I'm surprised she got out a whole sentence.

"You are," I say. "You're my adopted mother." I hate it when she does this.

"Oh, I see. Who's your—?"

"You mean my birth mother? I never got to meet her." My throat snags around the words.

"*Is that right?*" she emphasizes in a sincere tone, completely unaware of our tangled history. Her spun-silk white hair hangs over her eyes. I hunt for the bobby pins hidden in the mass of soft curls and pin her hair into a loose French twist like she wore when I was a child, when her hair was a tower. She grabs the bowl of banana pudding off the tray and eats her dessert while I pin.

"How did I get you? What I mean to say is… who…?" She looks at me as if I'm a casual acquaintance to pass a pleasant meal with, her face drawn tight in an animated smile.

"Mother, don't you remember? Dr. Clark told you that my grandmother was looking for a good home for me. Remember? He brought you down to Florida, and you came and got me in his black limousine, remember?"

I kneel in front of her and tell her the story of how we met. And though

I know she can't hold onto the words for very long, I tell her anyway. Not for her—for me.

Fantasies

There are times when my frustration and desperation have only one outlet—fantasies. I am not proud of these, but I am proud that I haven't attempted to carry them out. So far, they have stayed tucked in my imagination. Like that little stopper that dances on top of a pressure cooker when the steam builds, my fantasies do the cha-cha when things get rough.

One recurrent fantasy is that I dress my Mother, load her in the wheelchair, pack a bag, much like a baby bag—diapers, a change of clothes, and a note that says, "feed her ice-cream bars only," and then I drop her off at the emergency room of the local hospital.

I've thought it out; it has to be a hospital she hasn't been to before. If she's been there, believe me, they'll remember her and trace her back to me. I believe there are only two hospitals within a fifty-mile radius she hasn't visited by now, so it'll have to be one of those. I'll tell her we're going to the hospital. She'll go for that, she's usually up for the attention.

I'll sign her in under a fake name, but I'll have to leave before they ask for insurance cards. I'll tell her I'm going to buy coffee. She'll nod and then I'll slip out…

The air in the parking lot will never have smelled so sweet. The crepe myrtle clusters will bob on the ends of long tree branches. I'll start up the truck and wonder, what does a person do with this much freedom?

We won't watch the news for a week. I'll tell the family it upsets me. I'm sure the story of the abandoned old lady will run only a few nights. Unless it involves sex, murder, a body, and has some political overtones, no story has much lead-time. I'll tell my family that Mother's in the hospital and pretend to visit her daily. Of course, those visits will be spent walking on the beach, wandering the aisles of bookstores, or simply sitting in my truck and dozing in the sun. I've got two years of sleep deprivation to make up for.

I haven't worked out the ending, whether they'll know or not know what I've done. My husband is way too honorable to allow this, but she's not his mother, so he doesn't have all of the historical angst I have, and *he gets to leave each morning.*

I know they'd eventually track her back to me, and the ending of my fantasy brings me back to reality, the place I don't want to be. I'd rather stay in la-la land, imagining the headlines, "Sex and murder in our capital. Old lady still unclaimed. Details at eleven." I might have to color her hair in case they run her picture.

Inventions

How come if someone walked into my living room and saw my mother in a playpen, they would think I was nuts and call the authorities? But if they came into my living room and saw my baby in a playpen, they'd smile, say, "Coochy-coo," and not give it another thought?

Mother needs containing. She doesn't need free reign. She needs a cage. I know, wrong choice of words—a pen, as in playpen. It would be bright and colorful and I'd check it for safety. Her toys of choice would include a play telephone, some purses, shoes, jewelry, scarves, bathroom toiletries, and an odd array ranging from paper clips to Little Debbies to put into and take out of those handbags.

I wouldn't leave her in there all day, just when I needed to get something done, like take a shower, clean the fridge, do my homework or fix dinner. I would place some of those unbreakable mirrors around the sides, add some educational toys, and maybe a rattle. No, I take that back—she's a lifetime banger. I'd talk to her from across the room and make her squeal with delight at a game of peek-a-boo. I'd even read her a story. I love stories.

I'm not trying to be facetious. I just need to know she's safe and I need to be able to get something done. Is that so bad?

If I actually do invent an adult playpen, I just won't open the front door. That way, I won't have any explaining to do.

Thrive

I've decided to turn myself in to the Department of Family and Children Services. I'll call in a report using one of those voice change deals you see in movies when the bad guys ask for a ransom. I'll tell them I'm an unfit mother—I mean, daughter. I'll tell them Mother's failing to thrive. That's what nurses say about babies who aren't doing well, when they're not gaining weight or responding to stimulus. I'll tell them we're not bonding.

I'll try and look sad when they take her away.

"My baby, my baby!" I'll sob at the front door for a good show.

I hope they won't notice the beach bag next to my feet, stuffed with my car keys, a book and sunscreen. They'll put her in a foster home. I hope they have Klondike Bars or she'll be one unhappy guest. I don't think I'll tell them she's delirious; it'll take them a little longer to assess the situation if they don't know exactly what they're dealing with.

They'll tell me I have supervised visitation privileges. Maybe I'll tell them I pose a threat and then I'll twitch. Maybe they'll get me therapy. I love therapy. I like talking about me. I'd love to sit in a clean office and read magazines I don't ever get to buy and drink chilled water out of the water cooler in those cone-shaped paper cups. I hope the person in front of me has some serious issues and they have to go into overtime, like a baseball game when the score is tied at the end of the ninth inning. I like those pictures that health care facilities have on their walls—the ones with uplifting nature scenes and quotes on the bottom: *Success is when preparation meets opportunity*, or something equally nauseating.

I might have to have some fun with the counselor, as she looks at me with a glazed face that only years of institutionalized learning can produce. I'll make up a humdinger of a story, like Mother beat me when I was a kid. Wait, that part's true. Maybe they'll give me medication, though I prefer to remember my pain. It keeps me from going through things twice. I might suggest rehab. Twenty-eight days in a serene environment with grounds that rival the Augusta National's will give me a place to roll down hills and get in touch with my inner child.

I'm more afraid DFACS will decide to give me a second chance, and

I'll have to go to court where a judge will review my records then tell me I can have full custody again. In that case, I might have to have a relapse.

The Little Black Dress

I've decided to go ahead and buy the little black dress. Maybe I just want to go shopping, I don't know. This isn't the cute little black dress you wear to dinner parties, but the *other* little black dress. Mother has had her entire funeral planned out for years. She's not only chosen the songs, the preacher, the flower spray and the pall bearers, she has it all written out on note cards—in triplicate. I've had a set for years, she has a set and there's one in the safety deposit box in case we both got robbed or our houses burn to the ground simultaneously.

I'm now grateful for her preparedness. All of it will be quite overwhelming when she does pass away: getting her body to another state, renting hotel rooms, calling the funeral home and florist will be more than enough to handle. Maybe it's just an excuse to go shopping, but I'm following Mother's lead as I begin the hunt for the perfect black dress.

This dress will be unlike the one that every girl should have, sensuous and approachable. The kind that's good for any cocktail party, although I can't remember ever having been to a cocktail party. A black funeral dress must be demure, tasteful, classy, and understated—something I'm not. My favorite color is red. Red isn't exactly a popular or appropriate funeral color. Phillip likes my clothes to have a hint of the "come hither," and I prefer playful to serious, so we fit well. I used to apologize for our sensuality but as I've grown older, I've found that the most spiritual people I've ever encountered have an air of sensuality about them. They seem comfortable in their own skin.

The other clothing item I need to buy is a nightgown for Mother. She has asked to be buried in a pink negligee set. She says she wants to look as if she's sleeping. "Who are you fooling?" I want to ask. I do admit there doesn't seem to be any particular clothing item that seems natural for burial, probably because burial doesn't feel natural. Mother has saved a gown for years just for this occasion. She has had "the gown" for as long as I can remember. I'd go back into the spare bedroom and pull out the third drawer of the chest and there it'd be, in its mothball coffin, waiting. I looked at it the other day, and it's faded; the pink isn't so pink anymore.

I'm beginning my search for the dress and gown because shopping a few hours or days after someone dies seems sacrilegious. I associate shopping with fun, and that just doesn't seem like the time to be having fun. Like a little girl playing in her mama's high heels and makeup, I need to try on this future of mine. I need to play these games so I can keep on doing what I have to do every day.

So, on my shopping list is one little black dress, dark hose, and sensible shoes. Oh, one more thing—one pink negligee set, soft, sweet, and easy to sleep in.

Well Enough

Of all my children, my mother dislikes Christine the most, and the feeling is in some ways reciprocated. Christine doesn't fake it. She's a little like my mother, although she might hit me for saying that. Christine is outgoing, opinionated and enthusiastic, but she differs from Mother in one significant way—she abhors injustice. Mother's prejudicial remarks drive her nuts and she despises seeing Mother manipulate me. I've noticed how all my girls try to protect me from my mother at times. I take this as a sign of their love. I truly thought there'd be some fireworks with them living under the same roof. Mother should be grateful Christine is here. She's in college for her nursing degree and she's already an EMT. She's the one I turn to when I need Mother's pulse or blood pressure taken, and to check for broken bones. She has the strength to help me lift my Mother and get her into bed.

Mother has always favored Christine's older sister, Courtney. Mother has no idea the fun she's missing. Christine's hilarious, affectionate and generous beyond reason. Courtney's equally wonderful, just different— rational, peace-loving, thoughtful, with a surprising, sly wit. I've tried to explain to all of them that Mother had only one child to love, me, and that was late in life. She didn't have a lot of other things or people vying for time and attention. She simply doesn't know how to love more than one. She's always favored the obedient, oldest child, the child who learned to play her games. Christine was born with spunk. I can still see her at seven years old, with her hands on her hips and her jaw thrust out. Maybe Mother got a flashback of me at that age, although I was more of a mix of the two. I learned to protect my emotional turf.

I've stopped apologizing for Christine and her lack of hugs, kisses and mushy sentiments, and I've stopped trying to get her to like my mother. I don't blame Christine. I envy her forthrightness. I do ask that she respect Mother, even when she doesn't deserve it, and ask that she honor Mother's place as grandmother in our home. Christine comes right out and lets me know when things get screwy. I need that.

I'm glad I gave up trying to fix their relationship. It doesn't need fixing.

To Be Known

In the past fifteen months, I've come to know Mother's likes and dislikes. She adores Klondike Bars and Little Debbie oatmeal pies, which she now calls brown cakes. She'd eat these sweets and drink a can of Ensure all day long; the combination probably has enough sugar to send a diabetic into a coma. She hates pasta, which she calls *passta* and can't eat anything *tomatoey*. She prefers rice to a potato, unless it's a sweet potato, and would rather drink milk—she calls it "sweet milk"—than anything else. She'll take a sip of my Coke if I have one, asking for "just a swig," and then tears well in her eyes and her lips purse. She'll sling her head from side to side as if I had just given her straight Jack Daniel's. She likes nearly anything with whipped cream on top, and I do mean nearly anything. She's lived her life off potluck church dinners with food stacked three stories high, the flavors and textures all in one conglomeration. She eats figs and prunes, not because she likes them, but to help produce a daily *bm*—bowel movement—with which she is obsessed. She provides copious detail that would make any writer envious of her descriptive abilities, even on such a distasteful subject. I've also found out by talking with her friends and visiting various senior citizen centers that this fascination with bodily functions is not so out of the ordinary.

All this I know because we've stuck it out. Not because we were best buds or even blood kin, but because of a deeper bond—a choice. She chose me, for selfish and unselfish reasons, but hers was a decision all the same. I spent my twenties and thirties being angry at her about one thing or another. Now, I enter my forties with a bit of hindsight, and I'm just too tired to hold up that "I'm angry at the world" sign anymore. Maybe I just wore the thing out.

Mother's every meal is at my discretion. There is a weightiness that comes with knowing that a person won't eat unless you provide the food. "Don't give me no more chicken. I'm gonna turn into a chicken—look and see if I have any feathers yet," she says as she pushes her plate away, the white chunks only rearranged. The only thing completely eaten is the apple pie and whipped cream.

It's a good thing she can be funny; it saves me from domestic violence.

"You make your eggs too runny and your bacon too limp."

"Why don't you finish your toast, Mother?"

"It isn't dark enough."

I try. I really do try.

I take half-eaten trays back to the kitchen, and then proceed to feed a family that prefers something less bland. The dishes pile up like tired soldiers.

Now I face a new challenge: more and more plates come back barely touched. She claims it's too hot, too cold, too salty or too chewy. At first it was aggravating. Then the scraping of plates into the trash or the dog bowl grew until I could no longer fool myself. Mother isn't eating much anymore. A few bites constitute a whole meal. I've tried sitting right next to her, encouraging each bite. She eats so slowly I can see my fingernails grow. I remind her again and again, "Another bite, come on, one more."

I could at least cook for her until now. I knew what she wanted, and maybe that's what we all really need, for someone to know what we want.

Gone

"I want to go see Roxy—oh, that's right, Roxy's dead. What about Aunt Sophie and Uncle Floyd?"

"Them too," I answer as I pick up bits of tissues and a spilled water cup off the floor. I make a mental note to buy Mother a few sippy cups like the ones you give little kids.

"Mother? I know." She attempts to snap her fingers realizing her mother's gone as well. "Who of my kin is still alive?"

"Your sister, Emma, and her children"

"I know—let's go see Brother Jackson." She's talking about her old pastor. I try and give her a few seconds, hoping she'll realize he's gone as well. I hate being the bearer of death. To her, it's about 1955 and all those she knows and loves are living.

"He's gone too?"

"He's gone too, sweetie."

"Did I go to his funeral?"

"I'm sure you did."

"I don't remember. Did you?"

"No, I don't think I did, but I know you did."

"I can't remember, am I supposed to preach tonight?"

I take two bobby pins and pin the top of her hair back so it will stay out of her eyes. I remember her hands on my head, placing the pins in an X to hold back my overgrown bangs.

"No, sweetie, not tonight."

"I can't remember. I have too much to remember; that's the problem."

Is Alzheimer's an input problem, like the carrying capacity in nature, when the environment simply can't support any more of a species and the numbers begin to dwindle? I realize it's far more complicated, but right now, I'm considering this concept of having to remember too much. I'm concerned about my own mind and how much memory I, like my computer, have left.

I am now my mother's memory; we share my brain. I keep the names and dates and the chronology of her life and mine, ready to whip out like a brightly colored folder from which I retrieve the stored information. I can no longer go to my mother and ask her to recover bits of my, or her own, childhood.

What have we stumbled into? I'm not a doctor, but from what I've read in medical literature, Mother's agitation and referral to the past as if it were the here and now is beginning to resemble Alzheimer's. I didn't know this insidious disease had already started eating at her brain like a tapeworm, gobbling up decades, and spitting out confetti of confusion. I thought when she moved in with us that I'd have time to fill in the gaps.

What's In An Age?

"I don't know if I'm ninety-nine or seventy-nine. Do you go to school when you're ninety?"

"No, Mother, school's over." It's apparent that I'm sick of these questions.

"Sometimes you act like you're ninety," she says, playing with a paper clip she's found.

"You're going to have a birthday soon. What do you want for your birthday?" I ask, trying to suppress my grumpiness.

"To go home."

"This is the only home we have. What do you want for your birthday?" I repeat.

She doesn't answer.

Chocolate will have to do. Lots of chocolate.

Letter to Self

Dear Carol,

So far, you've been taking care of your mother for a year and a half. You've stuck it out through crazy times, angry times, tender times, through hospital visits and home health visits and while everyone else gets to come and go, you've stayed. You haven't had a vacation and no more than two days away this whole time.

I know that when your mother dies, you're going to feel guilty. I know you. You're going to think that you should have been kinder, less rushed, that you should have done more with her, taken her more places, insisted the kids be nicer. I know you're going to miss her and wish that a million things had been different.

I want you to know you did the best you could.

You remained faithful. You grappled with every decision. You let her into your life and your home, and you and your family did what most people wouldn't even have considered, much less done. People aren't perfect, and if they try to be, then they're not real. We're not supposed to get it all right.

Remember that you had to balance this with being a wife and mother. It's only natural to want to move forward and be more interested in your children, in those who are living. That's how the human race survives.

Remember that her emotions were always on an ever-widening pendulum and Alzheimer's took it to frightening heights and devastating lows. You learned as a child that you couldn't trust her with your heart although you kept trying. It just wasn't ever possible. That's okay. You also know she loved you. And you loved her.

So go, love your children. Love your husband. Live life. Learn and grow and help others. Let it go.

Remember all the kindnesses—how Phillip built her apartment and put up her pictures, whatnots and books, how you tried to make it as much like home as you could, even before you did your own home. Remember stopping just to buy Klondike Bars. Remember the hot washcloths and how good she said they felt. Remember kissing her goodnight on her forehead, and holding hands in the car, and how much she loved getting her toes done. Remember how much she made you laugh and cry and want to scream.

You always knew you were alive with her.

Remember.

First Fears

Mother's fearfulness is getting out of control. I came home from a quick trip to the store for toilet paper and milk to find a fire truck in my driveway. Three blue-uniformed men stood around Mother at the dining room table, chatting as casually as if they were all old friends.

"Your mother called us because she thought she heard an intruder. We checked the place out." The older one told me.

I cringed when I thought of my unmade bed, overflowing clothes hamper, sink full of dishes, any and all flat surfaces piled high with books and papers and coffee cups.

They left. I asked her what happened. She said she heard the doorbell. I told her robbers rarely bother ringing the doorbell. She said they might. I went outside and found a small FedEx package next to a flowerpot. I put the toilet paper away and started cleaning, in case the postman had a delivery.

Mother's fears are exploding. I can't keep up with them. I'm running around all day long trying to calm her. Threats of robbers, hearing strange sounds, fear of falling, of dying; even her fear of being left alone for a few minutes is out of control. I'm not a natural worrywart, and this wears against my grain.

Each portion of the day seems to reveal another fear. Even her faith in God doesn't seem to dissipate these irrational concerns. She's read the Bible through every year for nearly forty years. She's prayed on her knees an hour a day behind closed doors ever since I've known her. She's attended enough church services to have some kind of record in the Dedication Hall of Fame, yet all of this does nothing to quench her worries.

Scientists say that babies are born with only one fear—the fear of falling. When a baby is born, a doctor tests it by lifting the baby slightly by its arms then letting go to see if it startles, if its arms flail. The startle reflex is a sign that the baby is alert and healthy. Are some of us born with an overdose of fear? Is it gathered in childhood from "nervous" parents? Do we cultivate fear throughout our lives, collect seeds of doubt and stuff them in our pockets, only to have them sprout into giant stalks in our old age?

I Need to Know. I Want To Know

I drive to the bookstore alone. I want to know what's going to happen to me, and to my mother. I want to know what it's like to die. I need some road map through this. No one will tell me. It's not like I can just walk up to someone who has witnessed the end of life and say, "So, how was it? How was it *really*? Give me a blow-by-blow description." But that's what I want, so I turn to what I know. Books will tell me, writers have an unquenchable need to explore and explain what others deny and ignore.

I pull down every book that I think might help and take stacks to a nearby table. Read and sort, read and keep. I leave with six books. *How We Die, Saving Milly, The 36-Hour Day, A Grief Observed, Summer of the Great Grandmother,* and *Meditations for Women Who Do Too Much* fill my arms and will, I hope, soon fill my soul. Part of me wants to wander over to the magazines and look at colorful pictures of clothes and houses. I'd love to fall into the fiction, the children's picture books, and oh, the travel section lures me with its titles of Costa Rica, Bali, and Prague. That's where I want to be—alive in books—but today, there are other things I need to know.

Happiness

I've been ignoring Mother though my care has not decreased. Her meals, her meds, her laundry all systematically get done with some degree of timeliness. My voice has not changed pitch or inflection and yet, I'm not here. I've purposely done this. I have to detach or take up serious drinking or the kind of medication you can only get if you switch doctors regularly.

I fill my daily quota of what Mother needs as if I'm checking off a list on a clipboard with an attached pen. I answer her questions, gather the dirty cups and put back all the hairpins, brushes, trinkets and trash she's thrown or dropped around her bed. I can do this all while I'm thinking about my next college paper, whether Cherish should get a part-time job, the line of a poem or my grocery list—anything that transports me away from here.

"I'm not happy," Mother says, lunging toward me, in a Parkinson's jerky move meant to produce some forward momentum.

"I'm sorry," I reply, grabbing hold of her arm before she falls. Something catches in my shoulder. I wince with the spasm and shift to hold us both upright. She doesn't notice.

"I'm not happy. I haven't been for a long, long time."

I walk her back to her bed and remove my husband's house shoes that she's claimed. My fingers press into her puffy ankles as I swing her legs around in the bed and cover her with an afghan. I've managed to put her to bed without her ever acknowledging that's where she wants to be. That's where I want her to be.

"You hear me? I'm not happy!"

"Would you like a Klondike Bar?" I think of my children's snotty faces after a spill on the swing and how they sniffed up their tears with a cherry Popsicle in hand.

"Yes." Something in her face softens.

I unwrap the bar half way down and hand her a warm wet washcloth and a towel to lay across her gown. I sit in the chair beside her and keep her company while she eats it. Then I go back to ignoring her, thinking of how she no longer seems to think of what's happening to anybody else. Is her unhappiness, or anybody's for that matter, a result of selfish thinking? I realize her brain may no longer be capable of anything else.

Mother's doctors agree that she shows symptoms of Alzheimer's as well as Parkinson's and heart disease. Alzheimer's is only officially diagnosed through an autopsy. Terrible way to get a diagnosis. I don't tell Mother. I haven't told anyone, not yet. What good would it do to tell her she has Alzheimer's?

I have to detach. I can't feel all of this all of the time. If only one of us can be happy, I've decided it's going to be me.

Expecting

"I'm ready to go."

Mother shuffles through the kitchen and flops down in a chair.

Her fur-trimmed hat is on crooked. She's been wearing it a lot lately. She's put a skirt and blouse on over her nightgown and is wearing one gold shoe and one loafer. A burgundy leather purse swings from the crook of her arm, draped with a turquoise sweater. "I'm not going anywhere, sweetheart," I announce over the noise of the television, still drinking my coffee in my bathrobe, my feet propped up on the coffee table.

"What? I'm supposed to preach today!"

"No, honey, you're done preaching." I'm engrossed in some mindless morning show and don't bother looking her way. Cherish comes into the room, still half asleep, and lies down on the couch next to me.

"Come here, child, and take-*theez-thanz*."

I notice Mother's words are slurred more than usual. She wants Cherish to do something, but I couldn't quite make it out.

Cherish gets up, walks into the kitchen without saying a word to either of us. She's inherited my morning unpleasantness. She opens the refrigerator and gets out the orange juice. Mother looks at her for an answer, but she's unwilling to decipher her grandmother's ramblings first thing in the morning. I usually understand Mother's garbled words, but the rest of my family often needs me to interpret.

"They're so mean," Mother mumbles, but I hear it.

Cherish pours her juice and sits back down. Mother starts to say it again.

"Don't start," I say.

"They need to..." Mother stops, lifts her head... "Do you hear that?"

I listen.

"It's sayin', *Swee-ty, Swee-ty, Swee-ty*."

I turn down the television, wondering what that noise is, then I hear it again. It's a bird. Its song is muffled through glass and wall, and I'm surprised Mother heard it. Cherish stops and listens too. We all sit quietly, expectantly.

"*Swee-ty, Swee-ty, Swee-ty.* That's exactly what it sounds like. *Ha!*" Mother lets out a hearty chuckle.

Cherish and I give each other a smile. It's good to see Mother laugh. I imagine the tiny creature, grasping a limb with its small talons, its chest swollen, belting out this tune. Mother's face is raised, all of her features held high, waiting for the next note.

"*Swee-ty, Swee-ty, Swee-ty.*"

Birthday

Tomorrow is Mother's ninety-first birthday. I told her yesterday but it didn't register. She was born in 1911; I'm not sure if she even remembers that. I hold her thoughts, handing her a morsel when asked, and saving the rest when it's too much. I bought her a cake, a box of chocolates, and a new gown. It's hard to buy for someone who's got ninety-one years of consumerism behind her and isn't exactly using up her belongings. It's more the gesture. I'll cook a roast and make some biscuits. We'll sing to her and hug her and take a few pictures. There's something amazing about making it to ninety-one. She deserves a cake and a song.

Desperation

"Give me the phone," Mother demands in a nasal voice, her glasses slid far down on her nose.

"Who would you like to call? Would you like for me to dial it?"

"No. I gotta get outta here." She sits on the side of the bed, breathing hard. She's been agitated all day. She tries to get up.

"Where would you like to go?"

"I'm *going* to go to stay with somebody else." Mother flops back down. "*I gotta get outta here. I want to go home! Why can't you just take me home?*" She grits her teeth, makes fists and shakes all over. She gets up fast and walks through my kitchen and toward the front door. I walk beside her, trying to think how to get her to turn around. Phillip isn't home and I don't want the girls to have to deal with this.

"Sweety, you can't leave."

"*Oh yes I can! Get out of my way!*" She pushes me against the wall with surprising strength and flings open the front door.

"Mother, calm down."

"*I won't. You won't let me go home. Mother's expecting me!*" She screams and shakes her fists. She grits her teeth and gets right in my face; her eyes are blank, as if I'm no one to her. She digs her nails into my arm, moans and screams, sways from side to side. All I can do is stand here and let her claw me. If I do anything I'm afraid she'll fall on this hard tile floor.

I can't think. I look up into the mirror and see me, see us. I see what we're doing but I can't *do* anything.

She lifts one hand, curling her fingers like a claw. She's going for my face. I knock her hand to the side.

"*Mother! Stop!*"

"*You can't keep me here. I'll scream! Somebody help me!*" She shouts over my shoulder into the driveway. I pull her inside, shove her out of the way with my body while holding onto her arm, then shut the door and turn the lock.

"Other than a nursing home, this is it." I block her path with my whole body. She's pushing. She butts up against me and slams me into the wall. She starts to fall. I grab her hard by the shoulders.

Something inside her lets go. Her rage is gone.

I walk her to the living room. She slings herself down in the chair, almost falling off the other side. I'm shaking. I'm remembering the times she'd lose her temper when I was a child, slapping me across the face. I push that out of my mind. I didn't realize that she's this strong. She could hurt somebody. I've left the girls with her. This is dangerous. I've got to think about what to do.

"I don't know why the Lord won't take me." She's crying now. "I've prayed a thousand times, I'm ready... I'm ready... I want to be with my sweet Jesus."

I sit down on the couch. It's hot. I can't catch my breath. I get up to turn down the air. I walk behind her chair, watching her. Her eyes are closed; she lifts her hand toward the ceiling.

"I'm comin', just as fast as I can. I can't die unless I take a knife…" She pauses, making sure I heard it.

I've never heard her allude to such thoughts.

"I've thought about it, but it's not right. I can't. Lord, you'll have to take me. I'm through with this old world and all it has to offer. I'm old; take me. Take me Lord!"

Now I get it. She got herself all worked up and started imitating some televangelist she saw. I'm tired of this shit.

"This is from my heart, Lord. This is my deepest prayer. I'm ready!" She wails, her arms still lifted and swaying the way she does in church.

I check the lock on the front door, then shut the foyer doors and lay two dining room chairs on their sides in front of the doors so she can't just fling them out of her way. The girls walk past Mother while she's crying and praying. They give me a what's-going-on-look but keep going. I pick up the chairs so they can get by. They look at me funny but don't ask any questions. They tell me they're going to the mall, and I'm glad they're leaving. I relock the front door and put the chairs back the way I had them.

I can't do this. I can't expend this much emotional energy and then bounce back all perky. Mother always could. She used to say, "I'll slap you down with one hand, then pick you up with the other." Then she'd laugh.

I never found it funny.

I can't do this.

I leave her in the chair and walk down to the river.

If she gets out, she gets out.

Beauty

It's hard to remember to do more than brush my hair and put on clothes. Most days that's it—that's all I get to. By the time I've poured my coffee, I'm whisked away by the needs of my mother, my children, and a full house. I forget there's a me. I'm a set of two hands, two feet, and a brain that tells these limbs what to do next.

I've gained weight; I'm not sure how much. I've gone up a size, and now my waistbands are tight. I feel puffy. I eat whenever, standing up next to the kitchen counter, even in the middle of the night on my many awakenings. I eat whatever's at hand and there's always something in my hand, when I'm tired, when I'm lonely, when I'm mad. Dinner is interrupted with getting Mother more milk—she's spilled hers. I press her to eat another bite, and then I wind up eating two.

There are seasons in a woman's life for fussing about looks and seasons for sidelining these issues. What makes if particularly unfair is that most of us are at our prime in our late teens and twenties and later somehow we get it into our heads that we have to get back to that. We judge ourselves and others by our looks and then wail with indignation if others do the same. If we don't bother primping then we're " bookish" or "unfeminine" or "don't like men." A shower and fresh clothes aren't necessarily good enough for a woman, but we fawn over a man who's clean and has on a splash of cologne.

A woman doesn't always have the luxury of going on cleanliness alone. It's not that we're all vain and shallow and dream of bouncing down the beach as a *Baywatch* babe. Beauty is older than glossy magazines, deeper than a construction guy's whistle—beauty has many facets.

There's beauty in an Asian woman, educated and serious, walking down the street in Tokyo in working girl's clothes, and something just as alluring about her grandmother, in her kimono, on a small island, pouring tea and humming an ancient song. There's something equally inviting about a woman saddled on a horse, freckled, with a tinge of pink to her nose and a hint of grime on her jeans; and nothing is more beautifully earthy than a mother with swollen breasts and a thick middle, with a toddler scampering up her lap for some comforting. Beauty is the buds of acne on a forehead of a spindly legged thirteen-year-old not yet fully blossomed.

Sometimes I see Mother's beauty, so crystalline, and other times I see death. I understand why people recoil from the elderly. This type of beauty reveals itself ever so slowly. I'm over the whole glossy magazine look. Beauty doesn't need a touch-up job, only a surface splash of color.

Confidence, ease, grace, and goodness are more exquisite than a size four label on the back of your dress.

I think of Shirley's beauty, her hands gliding across Mother's back, the way she pinned Mother's hair in an elegant French Twist; then those same hands driving down the road, digging in a pickle jar. "We all get the face we deserve" is a quote that has stuck with me. I'm seeing beauty in the most unlikely of places—in the way Mother folds her hands one over the other or the way her laughter catches me off guard, and now I'm beginning to see this newly defined beauty in my own tiny wrinkles and sprouts of gray hair. I stand at the counter today and eat my ham sandwich. I know I don't need the chips. I won't stay this way, barely brushed, my waistband digging into my sides, but for now, I allow this world of my mother to define me. I tell myself it's not forever.

The Help

"You like to do this?" Mother asks me as I'm making her bed. "Hey, you like to do this?" she repeats.

She doesn't have the strength to sit up in her chair. She droops to one side, so I take two pillows and prop her up. She eats her angel food cake and whipped cream but only picks at the chicken and dumplings. This has been one rough week. I strip the acrid sheets and afghan, gather anything dirty or smelly and set two loads in front of the washer.

"Do you like to do this line of work?" she repeats again.

So now I'm the hired help.

"No, I don't." I tuck in the thermal blanket and move on to the pillows.

"Why do you do it then?"

"Because you're family and you need me."

I must amuse her.

A few minutes later she adds, "Does the state pay you?"

"I don't get paid."

"You don't? *Well, my goodness.*" She thinks a little more. "Who gives you your spending money?"

I hunt for trash and cups under her bed and make yet another mental note to buy a sippy cup and more carpet cleaner. I empty her porta-potty. Her urine is brown due to her medication, but I wonder if she's bleeding again.

"Hey!" She demands her help to answer.

"Phillip, I guess." I wonder if she remembers her question or who Phillip even is.

"Well, hand me my pocket book and I'll give you twenty-five dollars."

That's quite impressive for her.

"Let's get back in the bed. Stand up straight, that's it, move your feet." I have my arms completely under hers; I'm hugging her and straining to get her to walk to the bed. Even though she has lost a lot of weight, her bones feel so solid.

"Mother, keep walking, we're not there yet. You don't want to forget how to walk." I lay her in the bed, lift her cold legs and wonder how many times I've done this.

"Where's my pretty..." She searches for the word.

"Your afghan? It's in the wash, honey. I'll put it back on when it's dry." I turn to leave and am almost to the door when she asks,

"Who's your mother?" Been here before.

"You are. You're my adoptive mother and you're the only one I've got." She doesn't get it. I only tell her I'm adopted because I think somewhere in her mind she remembers she didn't have any children of her own. I turn off her bedroom light and turn on the small lamp in her living room, then go to her bed to kiss her good-night.

"Did your mother die?"

"Yes, she died," I say, and crumple up an ice-cream wrapper I've found under some papers and throw it in the trash.

"Is that right...?"

"Good-night, Mother. I'll check on you in a little while." I give her a kiss, feeling the lines of her dry forehead on my lips.

"Okay. Thanks for your help. You come back soon."

"I will, I will."

Lost

"Don't leave me," Mother begs as I hand her her afternoon medication.

"I'm just going to the kitchen, Mother. I've got to start dinner."

"Please, take me with you." She reaches out her hand for my pant leg and holds on.

"Honey, I'm not leaving the house."

"Are you going to church tonight?"

"No, there's no church tonight, it's Thursday. I'm just going to go start dinner, okay?" I try to open her fingers from around the cloth. She's got a good lock on it. As soon as I get one finger loose, she grabs hold of my hand.

"That girl said she'd be right back. Tell her to come and take me home."

"There's no other girl, honey, there's *only* me, and we *are* home." She lets go and gets quiet. I get so, so tired of saying this. I walk out her bedroom door.

"I'm so lost. You don't know what it's like to feel lost," she says, her words tinged with sorrow.

I stop, go and sit on the edge of her bed. We sit, silent.

"I promise, I'm right here and I won't leave you."

I let her feel my presence. No one could describe Alzheimer's better than this.

She's lost inside her own mind.

How cruel. How fucking cruel.

Part III

To confront a person with his own shadow
is to show him his own light.

Carl G. Jung

Empty Beds

Mother makes it all the way back to my bedroom. It's been a while since she's walked this far. When we first moved in here, she'd barge in, sending Phillip and me scrambling for cover. I wake up this morning to the twist of the door handle and I reach for the sheet. I'm naked and Phillip has just left for work a few minutes ago.

"It's still early, Mother. I'll make your breakfast and bring your medicine back to your room in a little while."

"I'll just get in the bed with you." She walks toward my bed, almost excited.

"No, no, I'll get up." I reach for my robe on the trunk at the end of the bed.

"No, I don't want you to. I'll just get in the bed with you." She sounds about four years old, reminding me of years when my children got in bed with me and I held them close, smelling their baby smells as we fell back to sleep. I pull on the cover while Mother tugs on the other end. I don't think she knows I don't have any clothes on.

"You woke me. I'm up now." I sound cold, colder than I mean to.

I can't let her get in bed with me. I can't explain why. It just feels weird. She left, disappointed, and I made her breakfast earlier than usual, anxious to stay busy, the whole time thinking about why I couldn't have just lain down with her.

Guilt causes me to fix her a big breakfast. I try to get her toast dark enough and her bacon crisp enough. I cook grits but the instant kind. I know I don't have a chance of getting the eggs right, so I scramble them with cheese. I drink my coffee and think while she eats.

When is it that we stop lying with our mothers? Who will we lie down with? Or more importantly, who will we not? Almost nightly, Mother asks for someone to lie down with her. Being widowed after fifty-two years of marriage has left her longing for warmth—a warmth I can't supply.

I consider myself a touchy-feely person. I can grab hold of a girlfriend's hand and not give a damn what others think. I'll hold someone who's crying, or give her a kiss when she's being cute and I'm forever hugging my kids. Phillip and I lie on the couch or the floor all the time; even in mid-day, we'll cuddle if the mood strikes us.

Does the issue of lying down with someone bother us because we are defenseless when we're horizontal? There's not only a sense of intimacy, but an undercurrent of sexuality, like it or not, in lying with another person. The Bible uses the term literally, "and he lay with her." Families don't experience it that way, and yet adolescence encourages new boundaries.

"I'm afraid my mother will swallow me up," my friend Debbie said when we shared why we can't lie down with our mothers anymore. I ache when I think of how lonely my mother is, how cold her bed must be.

I get Mother fed and back in her own bed, then go back to mine. Christine comes in later. She has just gotten out of her own bed wearing a long t-shirt and purple striped underwear, so fresh and young. She plops on the end of my bed with me and we lie on our bellies, covered by a quilt, our heads propped on pillows as we watch Good Morning America. Our coffee cups sit side by side in front of us on the trunk. It's one of those moments I tuck away in my mind so it will linger, unchanged.

I cringe to think of the time when my children can't or won't lie down with me if I am left alone in an empty bed.

Romance

One of my girls commented that she wanted a man more romantic than her dad. Romance is a sneaky thing. People go for the obvious. It's like God. We tend to think if we own a Bible and show up at church that it constitutes a relationship and says to the world we know who "He" is. God is not so easily defined and neither is romance. Romance isn't a pre-described checklist of a dozen roses and a dinner reservation. Romance surprises you, taps you on the back when you're least expecting it and takes your breath—much like the Divine.

Romance isn't all mush either. It's Phillip sticking with me for twenty-three years and putting up with my sniveling, I-had-a-bad-childhood, poor-me-I-was-adopted attitude, for tolerating all of the bounced check notices when I didn't fill out the register, and the thousands of misunderstandings and female tirades he's lived through. Then there are the real problems, the deep wounds any real marriage endures.

I would say to my daughter that this has been our most romantic year ever, from which reason and logic would recoil. Romance is wholeheartedly agreeing and insisting that my mother move in with us. Mother didn't much care for Phillip in the beginning because he didn't dazzle her with copious compliments, but she grew to respect him. Romance is telling his company he needs to take extra time to move his mother-in-law. It's spending three weeks in Florida alone, with his family in Atlanta. It's working all day, then coming home to sheetrock, mud, sand, paint, and doors to hang. It's working until midnight, trying to get mother's apartment ready—only to have her move in and tell everyone what she gave up.

Now that we've moved in, Mother monopolizes my time and attention to the point where I'm either in a zombie-trance from lack of sleep, or hysterical from being so mad I could spit. We can't take a shower or make love or have a quiet conversation without her barging in or calling me. I even have to wake him up in the middle of the night so he can help me get her back to bed, then hold me and tell me I'm doing the right thing.

Romance is Phillip attempting to reason with an Alzheimer's patient at five in the morning, walking her out of the bushes and back into the house, then dressing and leaving for work because he can't go back to sleep. Romance is rubbing my back in the shower while I hog all the hot water, then drying me and kissing my nose and wrapping me in the big fluffy towel and taking the thin one.

Romance is Phillip staying home with my mother while I take the girls to a movie because we can't all go at the same time. It's running out of her room coughing and gagging because she's had an "accident." Romance is coming home from work at ten in the morning, lifting her entire body off the floor, and then going back to work, repeating this at least once a month for months on end, never complaining, always gentle, speaking to all of us in that mellow daddy tone when we're all fighting. It's calling her "Mom"—a name that must be earned.

That's romance, at least the romance I'm living. In the past eighteen months, my husband has become the most attractive man on earth. I want to kiss him a thousand times and let my grateful tears mingle with those kisses.

Letter to Mother

Dear Mother,

I never wanted it to turn out this way. You, lost in confusion; me, overwhelmed and lost as to how to reach you. When you moved in with us, I was naïve enough to envision us sitting by the river, me holding your hand, you nestled under a lap blanket, and the two of us sharing memories of my childhood and your childhood. Somewhere in this idyllic dream, you'd doze. I'd feel the pressure of your hand loosen and I'd know you were gone. I would kiss your forehead and whisper, "I love you," as you began your journey home.

A fairy tale, I know.

The reality is that I tiptoe into your room each morning and hold my breath, watching for the rise of your chest. Not that I want you to die, rather that I fear that you have. Your life seems futile. Your days consist of not much more than a series of actions and reactions. Are you now more driven by instinct? Do hunger and thirst and a need to be covered up and warm, rule you in your wordless world? Am I trying to decide if your life is more or less valuable than mine?

Who am I to say?

Does this sound cruel? I don't mean it to.

I wake each morning to view the remnants of your destructive night. I pick up the nightstand, the telephone that is no longer plugged in. There's a mound of clothes on the end of your bed that you've taken off the hangers. More work for me. You've taken everything off. Your skin is as white as the whole milk you drink, but your eyes remain closed, shunning this world.

I thought you'd be different. I thought I'd be different. I didn't expect this. I miss you. I miss what little we had. I miss your humor, your laughter. You still laugh sometimes.

"Integrity is what you do when no one's looking." I wonder how I hold up to that definition. It's not that I do cruel things. It's that I don't seem to be able to relax, to sit down with you, talk, read the Bible to you. I'm scared, so I just stay on my feet. Part of me wants to help you make a scrapbook, watch some old TV show, anything that brings you a bit of pleasure. But it's too late. Those things no longer mean anything to you. Each day seems to pass and my family needs me, and you need me. I want to write, go for a walk, clean out the refrigerator, take a bath, anything to avoid you.

I haven't put you in diapers yet. You wet everything, and yet at least you still try to use the potty chair. I just can't do that to you—or me. I'm afraid the diapers will give you permission to give up. I know that day is coming, and I'm helpless to stop it, just another step in your descending world.

I tell you I love you, especially at night. I try not to let a night go by without telling you. I guess what I resent the most is the longevity of the situation. It's easy to be kind, loving and caring when there's a cut-off date. Cancer often makes people valiant. Families rally around loved ones, and last wishes get fulfilled, but this just seems to run into oblivion. I fear the possibility of years of your existence, staring off into space, and randomly screaming while I change your diapers, sheets and nightgowns, wondering why.

Still, I love you. I love that you loved me. I love that I had a mother.

If you could hear me, understand me and step back to see this whole picture of our lives, I think you'd be proud of me—of us.

We've made a good family.

Birthday

I turn forty-one today; I don't think I'll bother telling Mother. If she knew, she'd offer me twenty-five dollars, but there's no guarantee she'll even remember who I am or understand such words as "daughter" or "birthday."

She's never gone in big for my birthday, not as much as you would think for such a flamboyant personality type. It took finding my birth family to realize that her ambivalence was due to not sharing this day with me. I didn't leave *her* womb that May 28. Birthdays are not solitary celebrations, but this is the first time she isn't aware. I miss her acknowledgement. I didn't know I'd miss sharing things with her. It seems like all I ever did was try to keep things from her and now that I can, it's not what I want.

We always celebrated November 4, my adoption date, the day when I was born into Mother and Daddy's lives. We'd go out to eat and she always told me the story, her arms folded in memory.

"Why won't people tell me who they are?" she asked the other day, as if we need to announce our names, relationships and purposes when we enter a room.

We'll open presents and have an ice-cream cake after she goes to bed. I don't think I can take her not knowing me today.

Letting Go

"I won't tell anybody," Mother says as I load her in the car.

"Tell them what?"

"That you slap me."

"I don't—I never have." I put my foot up on the ledge and look her in the eye. She's hitting a sore spot and I'm no longer the cowering child.

"You slapped me twice yesterday."

"Mother, I have never, ever slapped you."

I think of all the times her hand has swung at me. The sting of her hand across my cheek. I need to let this go. It was so long ago, yet I still feel her slap. I'm grown. I need to get over this. It was a different era. Parents spanked, parents whipped. I know what it's like to say the wrong thing, do the wrong thing, only to feel as if it will never be forgotten. I've never slapped my children, but I'm not fool enough to think that's the only way to hurt a child. What are they holding on to?

Let it go, I whisper to all of us.

Nancy, Michael and Me

I carry on imaginary conversations with Nancy Reagan, Michael J. Fox, and Rosalyn Carter. We're all in a support group together. Nancy, Rosalyn and I are there, with Styrofoam cups of weak coffee in our hands. We're crying and complaining about not being able to sleep even when our sleep isn't interrupted and how we can't concentrate enough even to drive a car some days. Michael is countering, saying it's not so great on the other side either. We all look tired, in my dimly lit church basement daydream, but we're there, together. They give me strength in an ironic way. Parkinson's and Alzheimer's disease, our common denominator. It doesn't matter that they're famous or wealthy. Disease is not impressed with status and doesn't cut you any slack if you're not so famous either. It just is. Still, I think of them in their homes, doing what I do, feeling what I feel, and I'm less alone.

So many times throughout the day I think of Nancy, tiny, thin, exhausted Nancy, whispering into the ear of her Ronnie, whispering love secrets, a language that exists only between them and their endearing and enduring marriage. I think of Michael and his wife, Tracy, his body in a spasm and her smoothing his hair as the meds kick in and his muscles relax under her warm touch.

They are my foxhole buddies. We're in the trenches and the sky is lit with an eerie glow. Our hearing is shot from all the bombs, and the pepper of shrapnel rips at our souls. Winning the war is no longer our unifying goal. We're all just trying to get through the night.

Internal Monologue

I'm sick of hearing myself talk. I pull open the kitchen drawer, grab a notepad and begin to write:

Carol, you have got to stop griping about your Mother—if you don't, you'll drive everyone away. If I were your friend, I wouldn't pick up the phone. Why? You'd be saying the same thing you said yesterday. Stop letting your Mother rule your world. You're giving her too much power.

Bathing Mother

Before I can bathe my mother, I have to clean her room. She's demolished it again, and for the last three days I haven't been able to bring myself to do more than pick up the trash and push things to the side. This means it's been about a week since it's been thoroughly cleaned and that's way longer than it can go. But I have a family, a daughter who is learning to drive, who needs to go to youth group, and swim practice and even to the mall. She's a kid and she deserves to be one. I have a husband to make love to, when we have the energy. I have college and writing and gardening and roses. Even if I had nothing to do, who would want to do this?

I'm pacing. I've poured a Diet Coke and opened a candy bar as a reward, although food is unappealing right now. I've gotten out the bleach, the roll of trash bags, the mop, the broom, the dustpan, window cleaner, and the disinfectant. I focus on the trash first, walking step by step: table, floor, couch and sink. Mother loves oranges, and they are the one fresh fruit she'll eat every day. I swear she hides the peels from me. I find mildewed orange peels in the oddest locations— in her desk drawer, in envelopes or wedged between her sheets in the bottom of the bed. I stop and wash my hands with watermelon flavored anti-bacterial soap.

I remind myself to look in drawers and inside purses. I pull out more peels stuffed in the toes of shoes and under chairs and in the nightstand drawers. I wonder how many oranges I've fed her. How could I have missed all of these? I pick up paper plates that she's taken out of the garbage and ripped to shreds. I make a mental note not to leave the trashcan in here overnight. I open a drawer under her kitchen sink and find all of the silverware she's taken, and balled up napkins and ice-cream wrappers.

Moving to her bedroom, I find wads of wet toilet paper. I go and put on my kitchen scrub gloves, in case it's not just water. I find more shredded paper and more napkins, which reminds me to check the toilet. She flushes things she shouldn't. The toilet seems fine, but I unclog the napkin she's shoved down the drain of the sink. It's soggy and mushy and my stomach turns. Finally, the trash is out and I set it by the door, take off my gloves and wash my hands. I'll vacuum later. Dusting might have to wait a decade.

I lift Mother, now mostly dead weight, with my elbow under her armpits for leverage. I place her on the potty chair the way Shirley did.

"I'm falling, I'm falling!" She grabs my other arm and lands hard. I grab the back of the chair to keep myself from landing on top of her and toppling both of us to the ground.

I strip her bed, gather the sheets, blankets, underwear, booty socks and a fur-lined winter knit hat she likes to wear lately, although it's April. I start the wash, scooping copious amounts of Oxy Clean and two capfuls of Downy to go with the detergent, anything to help. I spray her room with Lysol again. I spray the ceiling fan so the fresh scent will circulate. I wipe down the vinyl mattress pad with bleach and then dilute Pine Sol in hot water in the sink, loving the astringent smell. I put clean sheets on the bed, the flannel ones this time, and open the blinds above her bed.

The ceiling fan spins full blast and the room is beginning to look and smell better. Mother doesn't like the light but it helps me work. Books and papers are scattered beside the bed. I reach under it, pulling out several spoons, glasses, a book, a framed picture of Daddy, a soiled pair of underwear and tweezers, which I know she wants me to use to pluck the hairs off her chin. She's starting to resemble Billy Goat Gruff.

I empty her potty chair and fill it and the toilet with bleach, then scrub them both and wipe the sink with pine cleaner. The different cleaning aromas swirl in my head, and I wonder if I'm getting some sort of janitorial high. I wash my hands again. I sit for a minute and take a sip of the Diet Coke but can't touch the candy bar.

She talks to me, but either I don't hear or can't differentiate her garbled speech. The words are nonsensical, and I've got so much to do. She tries to get up, but I ask her to sit back down and tell her I'm almost done. I pick up hair clips, a slip and camisole, an old photograph all rubber banded together with a magnifying glass on the outside. Daddy's pocket watch, and a dozen other objects are in a pile on top of the dresser. This morning, when I came into her room, I found one shoe propped up in each of the nine drawers, as if some poltergeist had played a trick in the night. I put them all back on the shoe rack and spray the shoe rack with Lysol.

I go back to my kitchen and drink my Diet Coke, wash my hands for the fourth time and catch my breath.

I fill a glass bowl with Dove liquid soap, warm water and a few splashes of Rose water. Christine gets rose water from an Indian store; it smells heavenly, and I wonder why we American women don't indulge in such a simple, heady luxury? I swish a clean washcloth into the bowl, drape a towel over my arm and go back to her apartment to bathe my mother.

"I think I'll let you bathe me," she says, seeing me coming her way with the bowl and towel. I wrap one arm around her body and raise her off the chair, trying to loosen and lift the stubborn nightgown from the backs of her legs with my other hand. She's no help. Aggravated at her random will, I shift and try again.

"Hey, I'm naked," she says, crossing her arms over her sagging breasts and small mound of a stomach.

"No one's here, just you and me; it's okay."

"But, I'm… timid." She laughs at her own joke.

"It's okay, I have to do this. If I don't bathe you today, I'm gonna have to change your name to Stinky."

She chuckles and I squeeze the warm cloth, brush back her hair with it and wash her face. She closes her eyes and I gently lift her chin, pause on her eyelids and let her relax. I let time pass, her face tilts up, the warm cloth soaking on her brow. I go around each ear, the back of her neck, and rinse. I wash her hair with the cloth as best I can. I'm not up to tackling a full hair washing today. I move on to her back and as the cloth glides down her marble-white skin, I notice how much her spine curves. The notches of her spine poke out and her ribs splay to the sides like an exotic fan. There's a hush—only the whir of the ceiling fan and the gentle agitation of the washer fills the house. I bathe her arms and let her soak her fingernails in the sudsy water.

There's something peaceful and holy about bathing someone, although I dread getting to the point to do it. It's intimate, physically taxing, and yet, as I surrender, a peace cocoons us. I scrub her nails hard, fearing where they've been and what they've touched. She eats with her hands more than I'd like her to, but I've learned not to fight her on something so natural.

I bathe her legs and attempt to go between each swollen toe. Her ankles are like balloons filled with wet sand. I lift her to her feet under much protest, take the dripping cloth and wipe her bottom, and between her legs while trying not to look. I hope I'm getting everything, because this is as far as I can go. She sits back down and shivers. I take a red towel, the one that hung as a guest towel in the hall bathroom of her house for as long as I can remember, and wipe her dry. Her eyes are still closed, her way of not having to be embarrassed.

Mother lifts her arms, and I slide the soft pink, nylon gown over her head. She loves nylon, though it's not my favorite material. This pale shade of pink is lovely against her thin veil of skin and silver-spun hair. I brush her hair and let it fall on her shoulders. I powder her, perfume her with White Shoulders, her scent, the scent I remember, and put lotion on her hands and feet.

"Do you get paid by the city or state?" she asks, and I feel a tinge of indignity, then decide not to answer.

I dump the gray water into the sink and wash my hands again, staring out the window, watching Spanish moss break loose from a limb and fall to the ground.

"Well, I'm gonna give you twenty-five dollars," Mother says.

I help her back into bed and lift her swollen feet together, then cover them with the flannel sheet. She asks for her afghan and I tell her it's not dry yet. I get a quilt and drape it across her legs and feet. She shivers and gives a soft smile.

"I can never thank you enough," she says, nodding off to sleep before I pull the cover all the way up.

Nots

I see Mother now as more or less a set of biological functions. Food is her drive. Her thoughts seem to swell like bilious clouds, deluge her world, and run off in the gully of confusion. She can't absorb memories, people's names or faces, what she had for lunch or what she's supposed to do with whatever thing is in her hand, whether it's a fork, a phone, or a pencil. She is back to her concentrated self. She is jealousy, only she can't think of the word or its origin; she is the little sister who didn't get the piano lessons her older sister did. She is the barren woman—who has forgotten her adopted child. She is alone, the wife of a man who won't come and take her home. She remembers what is not. I wonder about the *nots* in my own life, and if the void that life could not fill is what I'll be left with.

Breaking Point

I didn't expect it—not today—the day I would decide I couldn't take care of Mother anymore. It's not really about how hard it is to care for her, but then again, maybe it is. I should have known that in the end the deciding factor would not be when I had had enough, but when my family had had enough. Cherish is in the hospital. She has a severe kidney infection.

It started out with a backache that lasted for a couple of weeks, and then last night she came down with flu-like symptoms, only something was different about it. My mothering instinct kicked in, and I told Phillip I had to take her to the emergency room. She was admitted, and for the first time, I found myself in the children's wing of the hospital, the walls decorated with brightly colored tropical fish murals, and a friendly, concerned staff. I spent day and night beside her, getting washcloths, holding back her hair and wondering how she had gotten so sick and I didn't know it. I've spent every lucid moment taking care of my mother. My own child needed me and I didn't pick up on it.

Cherish's medications worked and we avoided surgery. She spent five days slowly improving. My mother-in-law flew in to take care of my mother, which was a godsend. On the day we were told we could leave, the doctor did a final exam. She asked questions I've never heard a doctor ask, like "Who's your best friend?" and "What do you like to do for fun?" Cherish's answers were polite, but lacked enthusiasm. The doctor asked what home was like and Cherish explained how her grandmother lived with us and how hard it's been. I sat there, stunned, not ever having fully realized the impact of Mother's care on my children's lives.

"Is your grandmother's care too much for you or your mom?" the doctor asked.

Cherish's timid nod "yes" was followed with tears and quivering lips.

It all fell away. The illusion that we were all coping was over. I admitted to myself, perhaps for the first time, that this was too much.

I have no right to put my family through this. I can't compromise my children. Mother's bizarre behavior is no different than living with the mentally ill. Its origin may be different, but no one would or should subject a child to this. Cherish has endured a worn-out mother, a bickering old woman of a grandmother who inflicts constant verbal attacks, and the loss of the freedom just to be a teenager. She has taken the brunt. Everything I've believed in is on shaky ground.

I don't know what I'm supposed to do now. I just know I can't keep doing this. I've been home a few days from the hospital; I pick up Mother's wallet, get out her insurance card and dial the number. Within fifteen minutes I'm talking to someone who suggests possibilities. Why haven't I thought of this before? What keeps me locked in the I-have-to-do-this mind-set? Guilt? Loyalty? A promise Mother asked of a child? I no longer feel obligated to do this no matter what. The *no matter what* is my family. I've done the best I can.

I've spent hours and hours over the last several days on the phone—time I don't have to waste—and I'm back to nowhere. The cost for nursing care is astronomical. Mother's conditions are not considered a "skilled-nurse necessity" and therefore Mother's insurance doesn't cover her. I'm stuck between paying out thousands a month for who knows how long, or piecing the care together as I've been doing while carrying the main load myself. So much for help.

I basically spent a week fooling myself, thinking that I could find Mother decent care without bankrupting us. So far, I haven't found it. Mother's been with us twenty months and I've done all that I know to do. It feels like it's time to let go, but I don't know where to turn.

Impass

I tell Phillip, "I quit." He says I can't. He says he'll try harder. Do more. The kids can help out more. I say no. No, they can't. We've all done enough. Too much. He says Mother's savings will be gone through in a matter of months if we put her in a home and her income isn't enough. Medicare won't cover it. I say I don't care. He says we can hire more help but we can't afford to put her in a home. I tell him that help doesn't help. It takes forever to find competent help.

I leave. I drive to the beach. I'm not mad at him. Yes I am. I'm mad at everyone. Cherish is recovering but I'm not sure I am.

The Other Bath

I walk back to Mother's room. She's naked, standing on the plastic mat I've put under her table. She's holding on to the back of the chair. I hear a soft plop and look down. Feces are everywhere.

"Oh God—what have you done?" I yell, not even thinking.

Mother startles, lets go of the chair, screams and falls back.

I just stand there, my brain shut off. I come out of it, afraid she's hit her head on the edge of the desk. I tell myself to go over to her. She didn't hit her head. She's lying in feces.

The smell rises. I run out of the room. I don't know why, I just do. I stand in the kitchen hallway next to the washer, holding my mouth.

I can't think. I don't know what to do. I have to figure out what to do. I have to think. I go back in and try to lift her. I can't find a place to stand. Brown mush smears the plastic. I'm sliding. I try to lift her by holding one arm. It doesn't work. I don't know how I'm going to get her up. I can't call Phillip. I can't get the girls. I can't call the fire department.

Oh God, Oh God…

She's muttering something. I ask her if she's okay. I can't understand her, then I get a "yes." I tell her I'll get her up in a minute.

I walk back out. Pace. Take off my house shoes and throw them in the garbage. I get on Phillip's old work boots.

I go back in. I can't think what to do, how to get some leverage. I stand over her, straddle her and grip her underneath her armpits. I lift her head and shoulders, then feel something warm pressing into my fingernails. I can't think about it. Not thinking, I get her sitting up but she's no help at all. She'll fall back if I let go.

I grab a chair with one hand, wrap my arms underneath hers and hoist her with all my might. I'm straining. I'm slipping. *Oh God, I'm slipping.* She's screaming. My shoulder feels like it's popped out of joint. I don't care. I take a deep breath, heave and pull.

I get one of her hips on the chair and grab her arm hard. She's moaning, but I don't have a choice.

She's on the chair. I tie her in place with the tie from her house robe. She's covered in brown sludge. It's in her hair. I go back to the kitchen, run the hot water, squeeze in liquid soap and pour in two, three capfuls of bleach. I grab two hand towels, three. I go back in, turn on the fan and begin scrubbing. I worry that the bleach might hurt her skin but I can't think of what else to do. I just do. I don't think. Not about anything.

By the time Phillip gets home, I've taken two showers, walked down to the river, cried, screamed and made three fuzzy navels—orange juice, peach Schnapps and vodka. Extra vodka. I tell him to order pizza. He asks where the number is and I point to the side of the fridge, but as I lift my arm, my shoulder catches again and I wince. He asks what's wrong with my shoulder. I tell him he doesn't want to know and brush past him with my full glass sloshing over the edge.

Mother is clean, lotioned, powdered, fed and taking a nap. And she's snoring.

Forever Lost

"Have you really lived 10,000 or more days, or have you lived one day 10,000 or more times?" I read this quote today from Wayne Dyer. Mother's room is a wreck—again. I spent hours cleaning out her fridge and bathroom, vacuumed, powdered, and disinfected everything only a few days ago, and now it's back to being smelly, dark and demolished.

This morning I feel as if I am walking into the madness of her mind. It's strewn out before me—the tablecloth is balled up on top of her dinette table, and she's sitting on the arm of the chair, which is a precarious situation. She clutches a pair of underwear, a wrench, and a face powder compact. She says she's ready to go. Her left foot is shaking hard from going all night without Parkinson's meds; her white hair is in her eyes and they are all but closed.

The placemats lie on the floor and an overturned tub of orange Jell-O with fruit cocktail is smashed into the carpet in front of the sink. As I walk into her bedroom, I see the fourth place mat on the dresser, a cup of overturned milk drips onto the carpet. I stoop to pick up a mirrored tray, dreading and expecting it to be broken, but it's not. The porta-potty that sits beside her bed at night has been turned over on its side, facing the closet.

I want to cry or spit.

Is she lost for good? I feel guilty for thinking about finding her another place to live. All semblance of relationship is gone except at night, when I put her in bed for what I hope will be the last time. I turn the lamp off, turn the bathroom light on and crack the door. I squish the pillows under her head and shoulders and remove her hairpins and glasses.

"Good-night, Mother. I love you." I put my hands on hers and let my warmth soak in.

"I love you too, darlin', with all my heart," she whispers in the dark.

Part IV

We understand death for the first time when he puts his hand
on the shoulder of someone we love.

Adrian Bartholdi

Protecting Mother

Something's shifted again. I won't, or can't, allow anyone to help me. I feed her, give her meds, bathe and change her and now even lift her off the floor alone. I tell myself it's because she always smells like urine, because her hair is in her eyes, because her room is trashed again and I don't want anyone else to see it. I don't want anyone to think I'm not taking good care of her. It's just more than I can stay ahead of. This morning I realize I don't want the bathers or friends or anyone to see my mother in this dark place.

I don't want anyone to see her in the grip of this madness that leaves her not knowing or caring whether she's face down on the floor or sitting upright, if she's defecated in the bed or on the carpet, if she has clothes on or not. I can't let anyone see her this way. In my mind she will always be stately and regal, extravagant in gesture and voice. Mother, *my mother*, would never have allowed herself, her room or anyone's room to be like this. This isn't my mother. This is some madwoman.

At this point, I don't know where to turn for help. I don't have the time or energy to search for it. My primary goal is to keep my children as healthy as possible while giving my mother the best care I can provide. I have to take care of myself and Phillip and my marriage. I can't inflict this pandemonium upon my family. I can't even talk about it.

Last night, Phillip commented with concern, not really judgment, as to how short-tempered I've been. I told him to back off. I was going through things I couldn't talk about, that I had to face this alone. He reached out his arms, offered to listen, to hold me. I told him no. Part of me is cold right now. It's not that he's not strong enough. His strength in both limb and soul are astounding. I don't want him to have to bear this, to have the memories I have.

Knowing

I realized last night that Mother isn't going to be here much longer. I had my last class of the semester last night. I'm glad I decided to take the summer off. The timing couldn't have been better. I missed some of my classes in the last few weeks, but the professors understood. I couldn't leave her.

Mother's stopped eating during the past week. She would ask for a Klondike and begin to scarf it down, and after the first two or three bites she would forget what she was doing. I fix her breakfast, sit beside her and wonder why she hasn't started to eat. I pick up the spoon and put it in her hand and she just looks at it. I put a spoonful in her mouth myself, and tell her to chew. She chews a few bites and stops. She's lost weight. I can't get her to eat, but she still drinks milk and I let her have all she wants.

I put her in diapers about three weeks ago, holding out for far too long. She's fallen again and again but has never broken anything. I called the doctor and he told me to bring her in. I can't get her in. I can't dress her and load her in the car, even with help. If a grown person doesn't want to be dressed, forget it.

She's not hurting or complaining. I'm not sure she knows what's going on. What good would another hospital stay do? An IV for dehydration? And then what? We were there just eight weeks ago They put her on fluids, ran some tests, suggested another exploratory surgery for one thing or another and then let us go, never realizing how they had mangled our lives. She doesn't need nurses waking her from her constant and random naps, or forcing food into her mouth for it only to pool and drip out the sides. She needs to be left alone. There's been such a change in her these past four weeks that I've shut down my life. As much as I know my girls need my attention, we all know we're in for the duration at this point.

This morning, I called a funeral home just to find out what the procedure is when someone dies out of the state. Maybe this is premature. I don't know. Maybe I called because it was something for me to do. I called the doctor's office and told the nurse that it was time for hospice. I've asked before only to be told that the doctor must sign that death is expected within six months. They always put me off, like they don't believe it's that bad.

It's time and I know it. I can't explain, but I know. I've had to totally re-shift my thinking—worrying about finding extra help or a facility is over. I called some of Mother's family members, her nieces and some of her close friends. I need people to know what's coming. I don't want it to be a shock.

The doctor agreed to hospice, but I resent getting help now. Where were they when I needed it? Where were they when she was screaming, accusing us of all manner of things, throwing glass, undressing and trying to leave the house? Now they want to come in wearing their super-medical capes and save the day?

I don't blame them, it's not hospice's fault, but why offer help only at the end? If she had had cancer or some other painful disease, I could have had help months ago. What asinine rule says that Alzheimer's families are somehow better off and can manage any better than cancer families? I guess their six-month time period is less predictable with Alzheimer's or Parkinson's.

I called hospice and set up the necessary appointments. First, a nurse comes out to assess the situation, then a social worker, and then bathers are assigned, then the clergy. Great. Like I've got time to fit four or five more people into my life. The nurse asked, "Do you want someone to come in and talk with you and your family about your mother dying?"

It's a little late, don't you think?

I'm angry. I don't want anyone getting between my mother and me. I want the quiet. Just us. We've made it this far. I don't want some stranger listing the five stages of grief they're reading off a pamphlet, but I don't want my cynicism to get in the way of what my family needs, of what Mother needs.

Now I'm sorry I called.

Signs

I walk down to the river, aching, hungry for God, but prayers are too big. Words don't come. The surface of the water is calm and the light at the horizon is faint lavender. Haze mutes the sky. I sit on the steps, unable to pray or think or cry.

Puh, puh—I look around, stand and wait. A fin arcs, separating the water, then a smaller one joins. They submerge and again I wait, hold my breath, and listen for theirs.

Puh, puh—A mother and baby dolphin emerge and exhale, following the line of the shore. Egrets, terns, and gulls squawk and clack, each adding its warnings to the others as the dolphins continue their slow crawl around the marsh. Tears come and now I can let them. I watch mother and baby, sleek and magnificent, powerful and joyful, play in my river.

God has never failed to reach into my world and do something spectacular and exquisite.

Comfort Food

I look at Mother's gaunt face and neck, the skin that covers little of the hinged ball and socket joints of her shoulders, and I'm no longer afraid. The anger and the fear have subsided, at least for a time. Mother and I are alone. It's June and Cherish is a lifeguard, Christine is at the fire station. Christine takes up my slack, drives Cherish around, picks up my groceries and throws in the wash. Cherish bakes me cookies and last night, she lit candles and drew me a bath. Without them, I couldn't do this.

The summer tomatoes growing outside are turning from green to blush. Mother does little more than sleep. Life has gone on without us and we're where we need to be. I've made the list—clean her apartment from top to bottom, buy the little black dress I talked about getting and never did, buy her negligee set, make copies of pictures to take with me to Georgia, write her funeral program. I've delegated as much as I can; everyone wants to help. The girls are choosing photos for Phillip to put in Power Point, so at Mother's service we can show pictures of her long and blessed life. They come home from work and go straight to Mother's room and see how we're doing. They hug me, full body hugs, and I draw from their strength.

I'm making chicken stew tonight. I need something homey, for the house to smell inviting. Maybe Mother will take a few sips. I put the chicken breasts, chopped onion, and garlic in Mother's old iron boiler, throw in salt, a pinch of sugar, fresh oregano and sage. I crack the lid and let the mixture come to a boil. It simmers for three hours, filling the place with memories. I do the laundry, sit with Mother, fold clothes, read Mother the twenty-third Psalm, make a few phones calls, sit with Mother some more, then watch *Andy Griffith*, hoping she'll rouse.

Mother lies on her side, knees drawn high, arms folded near her head. She's been like this for four or five days now. I gently roll her over every few hours. She's never had one bedsore. I check for them now. I need to be reassured that I've done as well or better than any hospital, nurse, or nursing home could have done. The aromas of onion and garlic grow richer, blending and merging. I chop carrots into very small pieces and a little bit of celery—not a lot. I put them into the broth then sit with Mother again. She wakes up and I lift her head to feed her the Parkinson's medication ground in applesauce. She isn't swallowing well. I give her a sip of milk, hoping it will lubricate her throat. She chokes. I wonder whether or not to keep giving her the medication.

I go back to the kitchen and lift the chicken pieces out of the boiler with a ladle and spread them out on Mother's cutting board. I sit with Mother while they cool, then chop the breasts and scrape them into the broth. I add butter and watch it melt into the stock, leaving round circles floating between bits of celery leaves, orange carrots and glossy garlic. I fill a large cup with milk, a little salt and pepper, and three generous spoons of self-rising flour, whisk it and pour it into the soup. The broth turns from translucent amber to golden cream. I mash a few clumps of flour with the side of a fork, then turn it down low and go back to Mother's side. I want a bath, but I don't want to leave her that long. I don't think I could unwind anyway.

I sit in the recliner next to her bed and read the one-hundredth Psalm out loud, knowing it by heart. I feel like a hypocrite. I wish I had done this more. Regrets are chasing me—I should have sat with her more, not been in such a hurry. Yet, I don't think I can just sit here. I feel such an urgency to get everything done, take care of all the piddling details. Part of me needs this giant list to check things off, part of me needs to do nothing but be right next to her. Back in the kitchen, I take a sip of the soup. It's good. I think of adding more spices but decide not to. If Mother's going to have any, it needs to be mild.

Hospice workers are coming tomorrow. I wonder if I'll say the right thing. I feel like I'm on trial.

Mother's hands and feet are cold. I turn her onto her other side; her hipbone protrudes, and I wonder how much weight she's lost. When did this happen? Should I have forced her to eat? Should I have called the ambulance? The skin from her forehead to her eyes stretches taut, back to her cheek in a sharp angle. I stare at her face, not wanting to remember what I see now. I need to trim her fingernails and pluck her chin hairs. Mother would never want to be seen with whiskers, as she called them.

I don't want to cry—not now.

I think I'll put a small Bible and pink rose in her hands, when she… She'll like that. She muttered this morning about going to the courthouse to get married. I hope when her eyes are closed she sees herself young, long-legged, and just beginning to live.

Requests

Mother slept all day, her mouth gaping, her legs twisted to the side. I slept in the chair beside her all morning, took a shower, and felt a little better. I spent the afternoon de-cluttering her apartment, taking down some of the many tins, photos, and whatnots that smother shelves and tabletops. Nurses and aids will be in here soon. It'll be cramped enough. Mother liked it this way. I always felt like I grew up in a musty old museum, not appreciating the artwork I lived with until I was grown.

Less than two years ago, I put these pictures up and unpacked her clowns and dolls, and now I'm packing them up again. I remove some of her "pretties," clean out her fridge, her microwave, make the room presentable for the hospice workers. Part of me feels strange for moving out chair after chair, dishes, excess clothing and towels while Mother lies in the room, still alive though sleeping. I wish she'd wake up and tell me to stop fiddling with her belongings. No matter what I bang, what falls or clatters or how loud the vacuum is, nothing wakes or even startles her. I'm not only cleaning to impress these people, it's so I can stay nearby and not go out of my mind.

Beyond a few sips of milk for breakfast, Mother hasn't eaten all day. I raise the head of the hospital bed she's been in for the last six months and straighten her shoulders. "You're killing me," she says with a scowl as I adjust her. I'm relieved and elated to hear her voice.

"You want something to eat? Some soup?" I ask, brushing her hair back with my fingers.

"A bar," she whispers.

I get out an ice-cream bar and a paring knife, pull the recliner next to her bed and cut off small hunks of ice cream. I try a spoon, but it's too clunky, and she isn't opening her mouth very wide, so I wedge the hunks with my fingers between her lips. She never opens her eyes, but obediently and willingly opens her mouth. Her hands remain woven one over the other on her chest and she eats without a word.

She eats the whole bar, her stomach growling and churning with the foreign food.

Cherish calls for me and I tell her to come in. I know she might be scared, or not want to come and I don't press her, but she comes a few minutes later and stands at the door, watching me feed my mother.

"Hi, Nanny, how are you?" she says.

"Louder," I whisper.

"Hi, Nanny, how are you?" There's a genuine sweetness in Cherish's voice. She glances down at the melting ice cream between my fingers.

"I have my good days and bad," Mother whispers, attempting to open her eyes.

I sit between them, listening, enjoying this brief moment of clarity.

"I hope you get better," Cherish says, and then pauses.

"Yes, hon?" I ask.

"Can I have that two-tiered table that's out in the hall?"

Duped

I spent the last thirty-six hours in funeral land—worrying, planning, making calls, and now I feel like an idiot. Last week, I called Mother's family and friends and told them I didn't think it would be much longer. I told them where Mother wanted her funeral. All of us cried, remembering times we had spent together and wallowing in our grief.

Yet today Mother sits on the side of the bed, looking no worse for wear, as the saying goes. Her almost weeklong lapse into a vegetative state appears to have been no more than a luxurious catnap—for her, at least.

She has no problem with being fed, opening her mouth and waiting for the next bite. She has no problem with my sitting up night after night, with my endless cleaning, neglecting my children, or the absentee wife my husband longs for.

Where am I? Feeding her ice cream.

Has this been some sort of elaborate dress rehearsal to make sure everything will run smoothly? If it is, it's not funny. I have a family, a life—I can't do this bedside vigil of wailing and waiting for weeks on end. I should have known. I can't tell whether I'm angry or just confused. Is this temporary or is she getting better? I don't know what to do or how to treat her. I don't know how long this will last. Part of me is really ticked.

She ate another ice cream bar this morning for breakfast, feeding herself this time. I'm going to the grocery store and then I'm going to clean my *own* house. I'm going to make margaritas with big chunky rims of salt, and fresh salsa and flaming fajitas. I'm going to play Santana on the stereo and dance around the living room, and then I'm going to go to my room, lock the door, and make love to my husband until he begs me to stop.

I've got to go on, for now. I've got to wake up each morning, dress, and care for those I love, including myself. I need to put on a dress, spritz with perfume and do the salsa.

I'm not setting up residence in Limbo-Land.

Do Not Resuscitate

I read *How We Die* by Dr. Nuland. Doesn't sound like a happy book, and maybe it's not, but it's well-written, tender and nowhere near the sterile prose of most medical help books. He writes of how we die from different diseases, and how in our modern world, we all have to die from something, not old age, not just because it's our time. We're into blame. I'm too tired to blame. I read his words about the end of Alzheimer's. So much of it I've already lived through. I read my future, take a deep breath and wonder how long it will be. I don't mean that the way it sounds, not completely.

The hospice nurse came by again today. All the preliminary work is done and Mother is officially on the terminally ill list. I'd like to ask the nurse where she was two years ago, but I'm sure it would lead to more paperwork. She gave Mother a number between twenty-five and thirty. Forty means you'll be around awhile, ten means death is imminent. Even as we die, we still have to do the math.

On the first visit, the nurse took Mother's vitals, asked questions, and wrote down a list of medications. I've been through this routine of home health care many times before. I nodded, handed her Mother's medicine bottles and wondered how long all this documentation would take. The nurse pulled out a stack of papers for me to sign. Across the top was written, *Do Not Resuscitate*. That means there will be no CPR, no doctor called if Mother goes into cardiac arrest, it'll just happen and no one will try to stop it. I signed all the papers then added the letters, DPOA, durable power of attorney, after my name.

I'm the one who takes this responsibility. I'm the one who must stand there as she clutches her chest and gasps for air. I'm the one who has to say "no" while others step back. I pray that I never have to stand there. I'm not sure I have that much courage or nerve or stoicism. Signing the paper is one thing, looking into her eyes is another.

So, we're here, near the end. No one knows when for sure, but we all know we're on the last turn of the journey. I hope Mother can let go of the tight-fisted grip she has on this life and reach out for the next one.

I pray that this will be a sweet time for all of us.

Coming Into My Own

I've heard some people say a woman doesn't truly come into her own until her mother passes. Perhaps it's becoming the matriarch of the family, assuming the responsibility and knowing that the legacy is yours to protect and pass on, or perhaps it's because of the wisdom and sorrow gained by living and participating in the dying of another person. I wonder why it's taken me so long to grow up, to be unafraid.

I no longer live in my mother's shadow. I've found my own womanhood. She's done her part to shed some light, and now I step up and take my place. All my parents are gone. The birth mother I never met, the birth father who I did meet—a man who never conquered his demons of alcohol and gambling; my beloved adoptive Daddy, and soon, Mother. No one's authority outweighs mine. And while this gives me confidence, I miss that backbone of strength and wisdom. There's no one for me to turn around and ask, "What was it like for you?"

Shave and a Haircut

Mother's back to her fetal position; she had a few days of being awake but weak, and now we're right back to this. It's been three days since she woke up and she's curled in a ball. My emotions are shot. I wiped her face and hands this morning after giving her her morning meds, which she choked on. I notice her nails—I've been putting it off for a while now, so I get out the scissors and trim her nails lower than usual, wondering if the next person to notice Mother's nails will be the person who does her hair and makeup after she dies. I wonder what she or he will be like and why you never run into a funeral home cosmetologist. Maybe you do, but they don't ever tell you, tired of explaining their peculiar but useful occupation and continually answering the question, "Why do you do it?" So they make up some other story, something ordinary.

I know what it's like not to want to explain.

I decide to shave the hairs on her chin. It's easier and maybe less painful than plucking. They, the beauty consultants of the world, tell you not to, that they'll grow back thicker, but considering our timeframe, I figure I've got nothing to lose. I'll try and wash her hair with a washcloth and give it a bit of a cut. Mother would want to look pretty for everyone. Her nails are better now, half moons lying on the nail bed, curved white tips. I place her hands back over her middle and kiss them.

Grudge Match

I knew that mending the wounds of our relationship was no longer possible long before Mother's mind detached. At first I thought I had missed my chance to make amends or accept one. Then I realized I'm not nearly as hurt and angry as I used to be. As Mother has grown too feeble to fight or even understand what we were fighting about, I slowly came to accept that it's all right, that even when she dies our relationship doesn't end. There's no need to try and hurry to make things right.

Something else interesting has happened. As Mother forgot the past—her name, my name, her own history as well as what she had for breakfast—she had no choice but to let go of her animosities toward me or anyone else. She can't remember them. When she let go, even for such a disheartening reason as memory loss, I no longer felt the need to keep up my end of the grudge.

Waiting

I sit here waiting for the nurse to come. I guess they're used to having people sit around happily or unhappily waiting on the impending death of a loved one. I'm supposed to be grateful for how wonderful hospice is. For me, right now they're just five more people trying to fit into an overcrowded bus. I know their organization is good. It's just that there's precious little to do now. I can change my own damn sheets. I can take her pulse. Yes, her heart is still beating. I'm more stressed out than ever and here I am, cleaning my house and waiting for them to show up. If I didn't have hospice, I'd have to call the police when Mother dies, as if I've done something wrong. Society, or the medical profession, can't seem to let people die at home anymore.

It's just a bad day. Here I am trying to handle all this and I just can't. I am so close to walking out that door. I want to do normal things—pay my library fine, buy my daughter a bathing suit, buy a rose bush and plant it. Just ordinary things.

The Missing

I'm not shaken by the fact that Mother is dying. It's a normal part of life, natural after a long and happy existence. People die. See? It even makes a complete simple sentence—noun, verb, compact and to the point.

I don't like death. It goes against my soul. Even though we live in a natural world where death surrounds us, it still seems foreign. It's the alarm that keeps blaring, *"Something's wrong, what's happening?"* Do I fear watching her die? Yes. No. I don't know. It's the change, the missing her, missing the routine, wondering what it's all about. The void. That's what gets me.

Where Are You, Mother?

You have diarrhea. I have to change diapers and pads and sheets and towels and you don't even know what's going on. You're curled up in a fetal position and when I try to undo the knot you've tied yourself in, you make a face like it hurts. I don't want to hurt you. I clean you as gently as possible, and then I leave you, one hand twisted at an odd angle and shoved under your legs. Your legs are drawn up toward your waist, your back wrenched the other way, your head slumped over. You're incoherent. When I ask you how you feel, if you're hungry or thirsty, you look at me through murky eyes, your mouth gaping, and you don't even blink. I sit next to you and write in my journal:

God, this is excruciating. What should I do? Show me how to do this.

Where are you, Mother? What's going on? I'm tired, but I'm more worried than tired. You won't eat and it's hard just letting you lie there not eating. The hospice nurse said not to force it and it felt fine when we were talking about it, but it doesn't feel fine now.

Are you dying? Is this it? Are you taking those final steps or is this just another dip and turn? I don't know; maybe it's not for me to know. I've been back to your room two dozen times this morning. I can't stay, I just keep pacing, adjusting your pillow and cover like it's going to help. I brush your hair back and look into your eyes, wondering if I've lost you for good.

Enough

Mother hasn't talked in more than two weeks. Not a word. They just disappeared. I tell her I love her. I ask her if she's hungry, if she'd like me to wet her lips. I read her the Psalms. We made our peace—I made our peace. I forgave and asked forgiveness.

She winked at me this morning. That was enough.

Where Are We Now?

Her room is clean now. I've scrubbed and bleached every surface. Everything is in order. I took out all of the clutter, cleaned the carpet, even put up a new lace curtain over her bed and added one of those sticky flowered borders around the top of her bedroom walls. I wish I had done that before but it wouldn't have been her room, it would have been mine. The nurse and I moved Mother's bed so we can get around it on both sides. We have put a draw sheet underneath her so we can lift and roll her. I've cut her gown up the back so we can change her easier. Her head is tilted slightly back, her mouth is open; it's probably easier for her to breathe that way, but the inside of her mouth feels like leather. I swab it out with water, then petroleum jelly. I've tried to adjust her head several times today but she keeps tilting it back to that position.

"Mother... hey, sweetie."

No response.

"Mother? You want something to drink?"

Nothing.

"Mother... look at me. Are you hungry, honey?" I turn her head my way. Her eyes move but she isn't looking at me or at anything. Her mouth is still open even after turning her head. The skin on her forehead is dry and her eyes are hazed and unfocused.

I wonder whether I should pray or sing or something.

I hold her hands. The skin on her face is smooth, all the wrinkles fall back toward her ears and hair. Her cheeks are hollow where her teeth were. I stare at her skeleton, lift her head with my hand—it's heavy, and I'm taken aback at how heavy it is.

I hold a cup of milk to her lips. Her lips barely move, but they do form around the cup just a little. She takes a sip, then burps, and then coughs up all the milk. She's choking, what do I do? She stops. She's so still. More milk comes back out the sides of her mouth.

I wipe her down with a damp cloth. It won't be long. I don't want to tell people again. My girls even told their bosses to expect them to miss a few days for a funeral and then Mother seemed to get better. Their bosses acted upset like we made the whole thing up.

I don't want to put them through another roller coaster spin. I really don't think she'll pull out of this one, but we've all got emotional whiplash. I'll give it a few days. They're good at reading my moods. I doubt I'll have to tell them.

Goodnight

Mother smiled tonight, smiled off to space with a big open-mouth grin. Something she was seeing, imagining, or thinking about made her beam. When Daddy was dying, he said that Jesus came and stood at the foot of his bed. He said that Jesus told him not to fear death, that death would be sweet. If it had been anyone else in the world, I would have doubted him—but not my Daddy. He didn't lie or play games or pull dramatic stunts. He only told one person, an old friend of his. I didn't know this until after he was gone.

I wonder if Mother had a visitation?

A Bargain

Call me practical. I looked up funeral homes in the Yellow Pages and saw a large ad that read, The Casket Store—Caskets and other funeral needs for forty to sixty percent off. I hate the name. How descriptive! I call the store and get directions. The hospice nurse came at four-thirty. I tell her I'll be home by six. Christine comes in with several bags of groceries. She says she's making lasagna. I'm relieved. I can't think about cooking right now. It's good to see her in the kitchen, her face so intent as she cooks the Italian sausage.

I drive in the rain and find the store tucked in the corner of a strip mall next to a home and garden outlet with stacks of outdoor umbrellas, chairs, urns and outdoor fireplaces. I walk into The Casket Store, being pelted with fat raindrops that sound like hail on the cars. Caskets line the walls down one side, up the other and a center aisle, all open—silver ones, brass ones, wood ones with cream, light blue or delicate pink linings. Some are inscribed with the words *God Bless*, another has a Veterans' symbol, another embroidered roses. I think of Wingo's grandfather in Pat Conroy's *Prince of Tides*—getting into the coffin to "try it on." I don't think I'll try it on. I walk around until I decide on "The Florence," wishing I were *in* Florence. I never knew caskets had proper names or could be bought at bargain prices. Mother's has a soft pink pleated lining and a large cushy pillow.

The saleswoman seems nice in a depressed sort of way, like she's being pulled to the ground. She tells me her own mother died last year. I try to comfort her, which I think is odd. I leave, after holding the casket with a five hundred dollar deposit. I tell her I'll call. I don't say, "When it happens," but she knows.

It's a dark downpour and the sky is heavy. It's rained every day for two weeks or more. I can't tell, I haven't been paying attention to how long it's been. I'm soaked. I walk out the door and glance at the nearby patio umbrellas and yard furniture. Everything is waterlogged. I can barely see to drive and the windshield wipers beat fast but do little.

It's raining as hard as I wish I could cry.

The Gathering

We're all here. Courtney's here, she drove down last night. I told her that this is it, and she came immediately, saying she didn't want any regrets. I stood at our glass front doors and waited to see her drive up. She set her bags down and held me. She's taller, much taller than I, and for a brief moment, I felt that turn of the tide; I was the child.

We cooked together, made a turkey and mashed potatoes, our own Thanksgiving. It felt so natural to be in the kitchen, two women, side by side, her checking the turkey, me stirring the gravy. There's something so comforting about working together, preparing food, taking bites.

I was mashing the potatoes and Courtney was leaning against the kitchen wall talking to me. It got quiet. She moved, like she was going to walk toward me, then stopped, then started again and came and held me.

I'll always have that.

Procrastination

Courtney stays with Mother and I go buy the dress. I thought about getting this dress over a year ago and never got around to it. A few months back, Christine and I were in the bathroom, sharing the mirror and putting on makeup, and I was complaining about Mother, as usual.

"Why don't you just find a nursing home, Mom. You've done enough," Christine said, putting on lipstick, glancing at my reflection.

"You know, one day before long, we'll be in front of this mirror again.

I'll have on a black dress, and I'll be fixing my hair and putting on lipstick and wondering why I'm bothering to look nice for a funeral." I stopped, put my makeup case back in my purse. The words were hard to finish. "I want to be able to look me in the eye and say, 'I'm proud of you.'"

The dress is knee-length, with tiny black beads sprinkled at the neckline. I'm finally here, with the dress hung over my arm, waiting in line. I've lived in this quasi-death mode for weeks now and I'm beginning to feel like that woman at the casket store—pulled downward.

I don't want to talk, I just want to get the dress and get out. I still need to buy Mother's negligee. It seems ridiculous to do such things at a time like this, but what's worse, doing it after? The dress is just a dress. I don't want to keep looking. It's the largest size I've ever bought in my life.

I walk through a department store looking for a gown and robe for Mother. It takes forever to find anything decent—sexy or flannel seem to be my only two choices. I finally find something tasteful in just the shade I want. I take it to the register. The sales clerk barely acknowledges me. My lack of makeup, my tie-dyed T-shirt and shorts must make me appear not worth their while. I buy the most expensive gown in the place, angry that the clerk spends more time with other women who appear to have more money. I don't know why I have to be mad at a stupid salesclerk, but I am.

Mother breathes in rapid chops. I can barely see her eyes because they're all but closed, and roll back toward the ceiling. I pull her afghan over her shoulders—she used to get so upset whenever I'd take one off the bed to wash it. She is just as I left her, nothing has moved, not even the finger I took care to put on the sheet in such a way that I could see if it had moved. I wet a washcloth and wipe her face, neck, and lips, then swab the inner lining of her mouth again. Her eyes open for just a moment.

"Good morning, sweetie." I wipe her forehead and hold the cool cloth on her eyes.

"I love you." I dab her hands, waiting for any kind of a response. Her brow wrinkles and she looks upset, as if she knows what's happening. Oh God, I don't want this. I don't want her to be upset. I kiss her and stroke her hair until the lines smooth out again. I let her rest. I decide not to try to rouse her again.

I wait for the hospice nurse to come to help me change Mother's diaper and check her feet. She doesn't like having her diaper changed and makes a face. She's still warm and her face is flushed. The booklet that hospice gave me says she may run a fever. I watch the rapid pulse of her heart beat in the dip of her neck, then smooth her hair.

I've always been afraid of seeing someone die, and here I am, no longer terrified.

Hesitance

I'm on this euphoric high. It's not real, I can tell. I'm not on any drugs, but it's that out-of-body feeling. I'm excited, hesitant and nervous about everything. Walking around feels different, like the balls of my feet are the only part of me touching the ground. I can't stop thinking. I need to keep moving. If I slow down, everything will fly off the earth.

What will I do? How do I start? I don't think I can handle more changes. I'm leery of what's next. I'm thinking about the funeral, the trip to Georgia. I see the cemetery, the gravesite, the mound of orange dirt, the chairs, the green tent. I see me, shaking hands, a long line of people streaming out in front of me.

I've been in this cocoon for so long, these walls are so familiar. I leap ahead to the actual death. Me, there, next to her—will she wake up? Say something? Scream? Will she grab me? Will she just fade away, not saying anything?

Suddenly I'm thinking about next year. Mother's gone. I'm still in school. Her apartment is empty.

I fell asleep in the chair next to her bed last night and woke up to her hard, choppy breathing. I had to get out of there—I crawled into bed with Phillip, pulling his leg and arm over me. I slept in my own bed from six until ten and woke in a panic, rushed back to Mother's room.

Courtney's there, reading a book—Mother's still breathing in hard chops.

The weather broke. It's sunny, with billowy clouds and a heavy breeze.

It's mid-June and I need to go do something normal but know I can't, so I send the girls to meet Phillip for lunch and tell them to bring me something back. I need to be here, in the house alone. I can't stay back there all the time, listening to her breathe, staring at her skeletal frame. I can't do that for hours on end without a break. I'm restless. I need to wash dishes and fiddle with things. My mind is a jumble. I can't form complete sentences or finish a thought.

I need to call the church, but it seems so morbid to do this before she dies—I need to call The Casket Store and tell them "not yet." It's the waiting that's so agonizing. Part of me wants to pick up the phone, call 9-1-1 and rush her to the hospital, fill her full of drugs like epinephrine or whatever the hell they use in those TV shows and jolt her back to life.

Then I ask, *would it work* and *for what?* It's harder, much, much harder not to intervene. I'm a properly conditioned twentieth century American woman who thinks that if I don't try some act of bravado to save her then I will have killed her. Is it not heroic to let someone go?

Hospice has a motto: We neither hasten nor postpone death.

But hospice isn't here. I am.

Purpose

I called the hospice nurse yesterday. I went outside on the front porch to talk to her, as if Mother might hear. I told her Mother wouldn't last much longer.

"What is it exactly you'd like for me to do?" the nurse asked.

"*Do?*" I'm flabbergasted.

"What is the purpose of your call?"

I wanted to reach through that phone and yank her up by her purpose and scream, "What the hell kind of question is that?"

"I just needed you to know." I turned off the phone and threw it in the rose bushes.

You know what I want? Here's what I want—for future reference:

I want you to tell me I'm doing the right thing. I want you to say" I'm so, so sorry," then be quiet for a minute. I want you to have the time to come here, and sit with me, and help me do things I don't feel comfortable doing alone or asking my family to do.

I want you to not be in a hurry. I want you to figure out if I need a hug or a cup of hot tea, or if I need you to tell me to go take a hot bath.

I want you to just be here until I don't need you to be here anymore.

I want you to not ask ridiculous questions and act like some yuppie psychologist who just got her degree last week and knows the right buzz words to get people to respond properly. I want you to have the common sense, the compassion and gentleness that ought to be instinctual, not only to a woman, a nurse, and a daughter but most of all, a hospice caregiver for God's sake!

That's what I want from you.

Compassion

The nurse told me she'd be out some time tomorrow. That's today, it's one o'clock in the afternoon, and I haven't even received a call. I've already requested a chaplain to visit twice. Maybe they're understaffed, underpaid and overworked like the rest of the world. But if you can't deliver on what you promise, then don't promise.

Maybe they do it all day long, day in and day out and they're worn rough like sandpaper. I don't know and I don't care why they're not doing it. They ought to. They ought to know how to soothe the prickly nerves of the family and give my mother whatever comfort she can receive. As far as I know, Mother doesn't appear to be in any pain, but I need someone here to tell me I'm doing this right.

I'm getting more compassion from my dog, Kismet. She comes by and licks me, lies next to my feet and curls up underneath Mother's bed. She acts happy to see me. She goes away when I need more space, then quietly returns and is there again just when I'm feeling alone. Some angels have tails.

Left

The hospice nurse just left. She was nice, a nice word for not much. I wasn't. She said she sensed "some independence" in me and that she didn't know how to help. I think she meant hostility. For some reason, this particular nurse just irritates me. There's another one that I find comforting. Maybe I just need to be mad at somebody. I know they're my emotional punching bag right now. She said the bather was coming today. I said no, that the last time she came, Mother cried.

I told the nurse that I want my privacy. There are some people you just can't open up to. You don't have that chemistry thing going on. It's no one's fault, but this isn't the time to fake it. I'm not trying to paint all nurses bad and me all good. Like most things in my life, the truth lies somewhere between the extremes.

The nurse said that the chaplain should be out today. I think Mother would like a formal prayer. I've prayed and read the Psalms to her and sang *Amazing Grace* and *Jesus Is The Sweetest Name I Know*, but maybe she needs something more than I can give.

The chaplain's name is Heidi. I hope we have chemistry.

Rattles

Mother has what they call the death rattle. Every time she takes a breath there's a rattle. Technically it's congestive heart failure—the fluid around her heart is building up and her body can't process it, so it's filling up in her lungs. I remember when Mother said she had that little kitten in her chest. She always was funny.

I keep going back to this book, *How We Die*, by Dr. Sherwin Nuland. It's been my Bible lately. He's guided me these past few months with his insight and depth into not only the process of death but its ramifications for the living as well. There's so little out there on how to do this. I need to know the physical side in order to grapple with the emotional and physical aspects of how to be with a loved one as she leaves this earth.

When I go to hold Mother's hand or lift it, it's lifeless. It may be warm, but it's deflated the way Daddy's was after he died. Dehydration has caused her skin to pucker and gather over blue and swollen veins. I wipe each hand with a warm cloth. I wipe her neck and chest, her cheeks and eyes, ears and hair.

It must feel good to her. It feels good to me.

No one's here and that's the way I like it, to be able to wander in and out as I need to, to pray, cry, talk, sing, and leave the room when I can't take it any more. I turn on the TV and hope for something funny, anything funny. I ramble down to the river and write, but I'm too anxious to sit and go back in. I'm going to take a bath. I haven't made any calls today. Everyone's just going to have to wait. I've done quite a bit. I just want to be quiet and let it happen, not make it happen.

Abandoning Ship

It's been almost two weeks since hospice gave Mother their official diagnosis, which might not seem like a long time, but I've lost all track of chronology. We went through several crazy weeks of her going in and out of consciousness and now, she's just lingering. It's beyond grueling. Christine's run away, literally and figuratively. She spent the night with a friend and came home about noon, changed, and went to the beach. She hugged me and whispered, "Please don't be mad." She's been here all along. I have to let her go, let her run. I want to run. I understand, but I couldn't show it. I acted cold—why did I do that? She hugged me hard. I didn't have the strength to give one back.

Cherish went to lifeguard and is spending the night away as well. It's the long, drawn-out process that's sucking the air out of our lungs. Courtney has to leave tonight and save the rest of her days off for the funeral. Maybe it's because she's here that the other two feel they can take a break, knowing I won't be alone. Courtney drove Cherish to work, made dinner, straightened up, spent time with me, with Mother, and looked at photos.

We've dragged out all of Mother's photo albums, pictures from childhood in the 1910s, dating in the twenties, marriage in the thirties, the war of the forties, all documented through her eyes. The girls have been poring over them, asking questions, and piecing together our remembrances of what she said. The albums sit on the coffee and end tables for us to pick up and put down. Courtney's going to take some photos back to Atlanta and have them blown up. I don't want this funeral to be about an old woman who has finally died. I want it to be about the life she lived. Mother's always wanted her funeral in a church, and made arrangements with her pastor back in Atlanta for her funeral to be there. I call him and tell him the news. Courtney's going to buy some candles for the tables and make a nice arrangement of the photos. We've decided to take some of these albums for people to look through.

I'm glad Courtney came, not only for Mother, but also for us, and for her own closure. She's become a woman. I feel this web of family, this new layer of generation unfolding. She has held her Nanny's hand, talked to her, and wiped her face all week—hard things. When she left, we lingered in the driveway and waved long after she disappeared around the curve. Each of us has found our own way back to Mother's room, shut the door, and made our peace. It's still raining. Three weeks now, I guess.

Heidi, the chaplain, came. She wore a lime-green linen dress. She talked with me as we strolled by the river. She asked questions and waited for the answers. She read the Bible and prayed with Mother, Phillip, and me. Nothing spectacular, nothing more than I have already done, but it felt good to hear those words spoken by someone else, to hold hands in a circle and for her to say that "God is in our midst." She told me I was doing the right thing. I needed to be told I was a good daughter.

Tangled

Mother's in a coma, though there's no doctor here to tell me so. She's been running a fever and she hasn't moved, not one toe, not one finger, not even the position of her head, since Sunday. The chaplain prayed and told Mother it was okay to let go, talking close to her head, her words clear and pointed, as if giving directions. I told Mother too, and yet we are going into day six.

This is unbearable. I ache all over. I can't eat or sleep. I've run out of things to do. Mother's spirit is tangled up with her will. I'm going to start packing for our trip to Georgia. I'm ordering the casket. I've finally come to that place and accepted that it's not cruel. The chaplain told me again that this is actually a very humane way for a person to go. E-mails and phone calls keep coming in from Mother's family and friends. She's outlived most of her peers, and many of those who are calling are the second generation of people who tell me of how Mother touched their lives, how she prayed for them and encouraged them in times of need. I wonder if my circle of influence will be as large. Prayers and thoughts reverberate around us and give us strength and peace in ways I can't quite describe.

It's the longest week of my life.

I sit beside her bed; each breath crackles and rattles. Her skin looks burned. I wipe her face and kiss her forehead. It's hot. I walk out for a minute to catch my breath, go outside and let the rain sting my face. I walk back into Mother's room and notice a sharp sweet smell. Death has a smell, a pungent odor that catches me hard in the chest. Birth has a smell, its own mark on our senses. Life entering and life leaving have their similarities.

I go back out to the river—ignoring the cold rain as it soaks through my clothes. I take the steps down, stand on the floating dock and feel its sway. *God, I can't do this. Give me the strength to do this.*

The rain pelts the river, penetrating the surface with thousands of needles, and the wind topples one wave over another. I remember the sun and the dolphins, and climb the stairs.

Angels Be Swift

It's six at night. There's longing in the air. I wake up from a fitful sleep to the sound of Mother's choppy breaths. It has grown even more ragged than before, with pauses, much longer pauses between hard puffs of exhalation.

It's here.

I stay in the room and don't leave her side.

She puffs, then puffs harder, then stops.

I wait, my own breath held, counting the seconds—four, five, six, on up to twenty. Then she takes another puff.

I feel her feet—they're cold—so are her hands. Her cheeks are cool to the touch. Her fever's broken, but I don't think this is a good sign. I wipe her face and hands with a warm cloth. Her eyes roll back.

I place the warm cloth on her lids, gently shutting them. As soon as I remove the cloth, her unseeing eyes turn again to the ceiling.

It's so quiet. I don't feel much of anything.

I pull up a kitchen stool and sit beside her bed. I can see her best from this side. I hold her hand; roll her thumb between my fingers, focusing on the ridges of her nail.

She lets me do anything I want to her, she has for days.

I don't want her to feel alone.

I look around the room. Everything's dim. I lean over and turn the clock so I can see it, and I feel this square plastic box I'm holding, its face of numbers staring back at me. The minute hand clicks, another gone by. I look outside. It's dark.

The next time I look at this clock, it will be over.

Her gasps and pauses are more and more intermittent—each one I think is the last, only for her to begin breathing again.

I pray.

Angels be swift.

God—don't let her suffer. Forgive me. Forgive us. Let only good come of this. Give her peace. Let death be sweet. Let her see Daddy. Give me a part of her. Don't let it all die.

I hold both of her hands, brush her hair back and lay my head on the rail. It's cool against my cheek. I turn my face, and let my other cheek feel this coolness.

Angels, be swift.

She stops breathing again.

I look up.

She closes her mouth, the most she's moved since last Saturday. She opens it, closes it again, and swallows. Her eyes squeeze shut. There's a slight gurgling sound, as if she's beginning to choke.

I get up—

She gasps again, another hard swallow, then a bigger gasp. Her head and neck tilt back. Then she stops.

It's over. I know it's over.

I wait.

She doesn't breathe again.

Her mouth slackens, eyes slightly open, but nothing moves. Her chest lies flat. The color leaves her lips.

I brush my hand against her cheek. Her skin is cool, just cool.

I wait, needing it to be only me.

Time passes. I look at the clock. 7:39.

I kiss her forehead, leaving my lips on her cool brow.

I walk into the living room and mouth to Phillip, "She's gone."

He comes to the doorway and holds me.

It's over.

Part V

In the sweet by and by, we shall meet on that beautiful shore…

S.F. Bennett

Keeping My Word

I call hospice. A nurse has to come to verify that Mother is gone. I assure them she is. They tell me it will be a couple of hours and will that be all right? I'm wondering what choice I have. I wait back in Mother's room. It doesn't feel right to leave her alone. It's a long two hours. I must be in some sort of shock. I can't feel or think, I'm just here. Phillip comes back, but can't stay. I don't blame him.

I've never seen the nurse who finally arrives—she's respectful and I'm in some out-of-body place. I assist her with a strange sense of calm. I help her dress Mother, shave her chin hairs again and ask if I can call their cosmetologist, that Mother wouldn't want a lot of makeup. I watch the two funeral workers load Mother into the hearse at 11:30. They drape Mother with a burgundy velvet cover and ask me if I want to leave her head uncovered as they wheel her out. They say it bothers some people.

"Cover her. I know she's gone." I follow them outside and feel the concrete of the driveway beneath my feet as I watch the gurney slide into the hearse. They shut the door and pull away. I stand until I can't see them anymore.

Mother—I saw it through to the end. I never left your side, not when the nurse came, not when the undertakers came. I didn't leave you. I never put you in a nursing home—I kept you here with us. I wanted to run, a thousand times I wanted to run, but I didn't. I followed through. It was hard in one way, but in another way, it's been the easiest thing I've ever done.

Sleep—No Dreams

I walk back to Mother's room; the smell makes me sick. I haven't changed her sheets this past week. I didn't want to move her that much. I stuff black trash bags with every sheet, towel, cover, and clothing she's used in the past several weeks—all except for her afghan. I take that outside and hang it on the fence to air out. I take the rest of the bags to the trash.

I need these sheets and towels to be gone. I spray the room until the Lysol can is empty. I leave the ceiling fan on high, with the light on. I can't think about anything right now. I can't.

I make a few calls, take three Tylenol PM, and beg God for sleep without dreams.

Leaving and Finishing

I wake from a dreamless sleep, already going over my list in my head. I make more calls, finish the arrangements for the funeral, and then decide to leave the house. I can't stay here. I need diversion; I can't stop seeing her face, her hands, and the nurse turning her on to her side and cleaning her body three hours after she had passed. She's white, so white. If I close my eyes I see the blue discoloration where her blood has pooled to her back. Why did they take so long getting here, leaving me with her. I can't stop seeing…

It's impossible to sit but hard to stay busy and not get bored with whatever's at hand. I ask Phillip to take us to the movies. I can't remember what we saw. I come home and the phone starts ringing. More details. I answer questions, give out our credit card number, check my list to make sure I've done it all. Family and friends call. I console them, they reassure me.

I can't feel a damn thing.

I was a coward. I just sat there. I wanted to scream, to pound on her chest, to beg the paramedics to come, and yet I sat, doing what hospice told me to do. Only today she's gone, and I'm not so sure I did the right thing.

Freedom

I can go out to dinner and a movie and not worry, not rush home. I can get in the car and just go, something I've missed for months and yet, what does that matter? What is freedom? Freedom is not having to walk back there, not having to give her pills or her breakfast, not stroke her hair as I walk by her sitting in the recliner. Is this what I thought I wanted?

We leave for Atlanta tomorrow, we'll check into a hotel, meet with the pastor, then get ready for the service. I'm so out of it, it's all a set of elaborate motions, one following the other. I want to do it right. I want her to be proud, for her funeral to be memorable. I want to finish this well.

Phillip anticipates my every move. He comes over and holds me. We go to the river and sit. He tells me to take a nap. I can't. He lies down next to me and tells me to stop being so hard on myself. We balance each other, him more cautious, me more excessive, us somewhere in the middle.

The girls move throughout the house like cats, gentle and unobtrusive. We meet in the hall and hold each other, sit on the couch staring at the TV, falling asleep, the one covering the other. Courtney calls off and on all day, needing to connect. She's back in Atlanta and says she'll get to the church early and she'll see us there.

All I can do is pack and wait; we're all just waiting.

Meeting Expectations

Phillip drives to Atlanta while I stare out the window, trying not to think. I've got plenty of time for that. We drive straight to the church. I write a check and pick out the paper the memorial service will be printed on. Phillip brought his laptop. He has scanned in pictures of my mother, all nine decades of her life, and I've written out highlights from each time period to go with the photos. My plan is to read my notes at the funeral, so that people get a sense of Mother's life, but we'll see how it goes. I have Mother's cards in my hand, the cards that tell me how she wants things to go. The date on the cards is 1988. She had written out newer ones but I found these first and pretty much knew of any changes.

We get to the church two hours before the funeral. We've decided to have visitation before the funeral and not the traditional night before. I'm afraid I've thrown people off—the church has had a lot of calls about what's going on. Courtney's already here with the blown-up photos and easels and candles. On one easel, we place a picture of Mother taken in the forties. She's playing an accordion and you can tell she's at a revival. She's smiling with those great cheeks of hers.

People pour in, loved ones from my childhood, Mother's church and family members, and friends I've collected. They just keep coming, each hugs me, tells me of moments they had with Mother. One tells me, "I didn't know how to pray; she taught me." Another says, "If it weren't for your Mother, I wouldn't have accepted Christ," and another, "I was in awe of her."

I nod and gather their stories, weaving them with my own. I feel selfish for dragging Mother to Florida for the last two years of her life, even though I know I didn't have another decent choice. I think of the last two years, of the things these people don't know, of all that Mother lost, and yet now, it's over. It's over, I tell myself.

They're still hugging me, thanking me. So many of these people are from my childhood. I kiss the faces of those I love, good people. I read her life story at the funeral, noting event after event and realizing, this was my mother, what she did with her life and the decisions she made—to serve God, become a minister, enjoy a long and happy marriage, adopt a little girl when she and Daddy were in their fifties. These decisions became reality and define and refine her. Each decade unfolds, revealing another layer.

It's a Pentecostal funeral. Someone from the church sings a fiery rendition of *Oh I Want To See Him*, and it feels like this is what she would have wanted.

I wrote in my journal today: Dear Mother, I hope you liked it.

Automatic Drive

I'm back home now and have spent several days unloading the car and tinkering around the house, not really accomplishing anything at all. I don't have brainpower and find myself staring, not thinking. I need something to do. All I've done is funeral stuff. I wake up, alive and strong, like a restless racehorse. I call insurance companies, answer letters, respond to phone calls and emails. I can't sleep without seeing her. A bottle of blue sleeping caplets sits next to my bed. I stare at them with caution then take one. I don't want to think when I close my eyes.

I'm going to get Phillip and myself enrolled at the new college; we're changing schools. I follow my list of things to do and walk around the campus, obediently following the paper directions from building to building. I drive up the driveway, home. I think about backing out of the driveway again. I'm running, I know it.

I keep walking back to Mother's room, compelled by habit to go check on her. Neither my body nor my soul can accept that one day someone is here, the next day, she's not. It goes beyond mere routine and has wriggled its way past my psyche into automatic drive. I miss her. I'm not sure I expected to miss her this soon. I miss what I knew as familiar and yet much more. I miss who she was to me. We had our differences. I've never argued more or got angrier with anyone in my life than with her. She could send me over the edge, absolutely infuriated, and other times she'd say something so incredibly tender.

My mother, my history, my childhood, she is—was—no, *is*—the definition of the daughter-facet of my life. A mother defines a part of her child that stays indefinitely. I miss her personhood, her personality, laugh, gesture, her take on life, even the parts I vehemently opposed. We fought it out. Ambivalence was never our problem.

Swirling

My mind is swirling with detail after detail. I'm waiting for the dreaded death certificate to come in the mail. I don't want to see the words. I'm tired of the phone calls asking for Mother—having to state again and again that she has passed away to telemarketers is sickening. How odd it is to try and soften the language: she died sounds so cold.

I'm trying not to expect so much of myself, to just let it flow, but I can't. I'm agitated again, forever leaning forward, lunging forward. I don't want to become a machine but there's an urgency to begin my new life that I can't shake. Death makes people want to live—live big expansive lives—to do bold things and say to hell with it, how long have I got anyway?

A Tear

It's the smell that gets me. Mother's apartment is still and clean. They came and took the hospital bed and the wheelchair away. The rooms sit vacant until I can find the momentum to pack and clean, and move things out so Christine can move in.

I need it to be something else.

It doesn't smell like Mother—that I could handle. It smells like death. That sickening-sweet odor overtakes me whenever I walk back there. I can feel myself falling. I see her, the last heave of her chest. I feel myself going there and I can't pull back.

Tomorrow, Phillip is taking the furniture out and I'm packing most of her clothes to take to Goodwill. I'm calling to have the rugs cleaned. I'm bleaching everything I possibly can. I've got to do this; I can't wait any longer. People tell you not to make any rash decisions. Believe me, I've had more than enough thinking time. I need those rooms to have life and joy and to smell of lemons and lavender. I need Christine's exuberance to fill the place.

I went to the beach today and played in the water, walked until sunset and collected shells. I need to infuse myself with the goings on of life. I need movies and sunflowers and long-distance phone calls with friends, and although I know I'm not great company and have a hard time keeping up the banter of a conversation, I need to at least be included.

I go outside and sit on the bench by the river to watch the sun rise and later set, hoping it will pull me along, wash me out with the tide, bring in fresh waters and take this sorrow away. I wake Phillip in the middle of the night to make love to him. I need to feel alive. I eat whatever I feel like—watermelon for dinner and midnight ham sandwiches. I'm enjoying commonplace sweetness. But still, I don't seem to be able to feel much of anything, no matter what I do.

Charred

About twelve years ago, I burned my hand and foot when I ran into the kitchen to answer the phone and somehow hit the stove. A cooked chicken and all its boiling water went airborne. I wound up in the hospital with second and third degree burns, and spent six weeks in debriding. Each day, someone had to drive me to the clinic where I had to slip my hand and foot into a swirling tub of bleach and Betadine. Then, the burn therapist scraped away the dead flesh, making room for the new. Each day the pain started over, the nauseating loss of flesh, and the woozy sensation as I dipped my hand or foot in the water. I went home with drugs and slept until morning. That was my routine.

The therapist met me at the door with a cup of ice cubes to crunch on and rub all over my face, hoping to prevent my stomach from lurching as I submerged my limbs into the cauldron. I remember it well—the stunned feeling—the charred, gray flesh that hung in loose chunks around my ankle.

That's what I feel like now, charred and ashen, beyond nerve endings and emotions, just a sort of undefined sick feeling, knowing it should hurt and questioning why it doesn't.

Historians

It's the beginning of a new week, full of promise. I'll be packing up mother's rooms. I've called the carpet cleaners. I'll play music while I'm back there, Bonnie Raitt, maybe. I'll open all the windows and doors and let light flood the place. I'm going to box everything up and not try to make any other decisions now. I know that would be foolish. I realize it will be the fall before this new life of mine settles in. I'm still waiting on the death certificates, which in turn means I still have to file insurance, close her accounts, and handle the final closing of her affairs.

Cherish is blossoming more and more. The move to Florida was hard enough for a teenager, and having this very difficult family situation to deal with didn't help. She's making friends this summer, and seems to enjoy lifeguarding and teaching little kids on the swim team. I see how much she needs me. She deserves a strong healthy mom, and not to live under such heaviness. I do think God intervened. Mother's actual passing was as easy as one could ask for, and it came when I wasn't sure any of us could have held on much longer.

It's my job to be the historian now, to hold the past and preserve it for the future. I'm well suited for this role, being a writer, being almost too contemplative, always gathering, a sort of mental pack rat. Although Daddy has been gone for nearly seventeen years, I've kept him alive. Talking about him is as easy as getting dressed each day. My girls don't remember their Papa, but they have a sense of who he was, who he is.

Something New

I can't go back to Mother's apartment when I'm the only one in the house, or when it's too close to bedtime. I had nightmares after Daddy died—deathmares is what I call them, those can't-accept-death dreams. In them, he's not really dead, he's come back half-dead. I was only twenty-two, but I'm not sure being young had anything to do with it. Since I lived Mother's dying for so long, I don't want to "live" it now. Even her belongings overwhelm me.

What to do with them all? I don't want them, not all of them, not every gem clip, staple, picture frame, plate, glass clown or teacup; each item triggers a memory and, worse, requires a decision. I never knew three rooms could hold so much.

Past Tense

My tongue doesn't want to do it. I'll start a sentence, some remembrance about my mother and I'll say, "Mother is..."

I'll stop and force a "was," but it's so awkward. Nothing in me accepts death, not my memories, not my tongue, not my daily routine. I just keep circling this pit in the middle of my life. Yes, I'm somewhat relieved of the work, the daily care. That's over, but it isn't—I mean, *wasn't*—so bad, not compared to the value of a life. It's hard to move to past tense.

I'll go out to the car for something then walk up the sidewalk and pass her kitchen window, and for that split second, I'll feel her in there; not just think, not remember, but *feel* her there. It's as if she's here, existing, so real I could turn the corner and she'd tap on the glass and wave to me.

Time is all jumbled up for me now. I can be four and fourteen and thirty-four all at the same moment. Mother is still here, not like a ghost who has unsettled business. It's a time thing; not enough of it has gone by, I guess. It's like a beautiful woman wearing an exotic perfume that lingers in the room long after she's gone. My language may reflect this new past-tense state but the rest of me doesn't.

Stepping Back

I had almost forgotten who Mother was. I got so used to seeing this shrunken version of her that I had forgotten the giant of my childhood. I lived with this preacher-woman, a legend in her circle of believers. I grew up being taught scriptures the way other children are taught their alphabet and colors. She had a whole life, a whole life before I ever got there. Mother had been an ordained minister for fifteen years before she adopted me, then went on holding her papers for twenty-five more years. She knew everybody and everybody knew her. She was on the radio, on television, traveled by train to other cities and held revivals. She played the piano, the accordion, and the guitar and sang in rich alto tones. I had forgotten about all of that. To me, she was my mother, and as I grew, she dwindled. Do my girls see me the same way? Am I already dwindling in their eyes?

I had become accustomed to this little old lady and all her eccentricities. I need to remember her whole life, not just the ending. I need to remember how she never stopped reading or praying or telling anyone and everyone about the rapture, how her magnificent presence almost sucked the air out of a room. I think I'm going through the part where you overlook a loved one's faults and frailties, almost idolizing them, maybe making up for how you thought about them while they were still here. I don't know, it's not good to analyze myself. There's not enough distance. All I can hope is that this pendulum of emotion will eventually find its balance.

The Dam

I'm crying over stupid stuff like the trash piling up in the kitchen, the fifteen-dollar parking ticket I got at college, and what time the girls come in. We all went to church this morning, something we had to take turns doing for the last two years. We had given it up at the end, not wanting to leave the other behind, and none of us getting enough sleep.

I can't sit still in the pew. I try to sing the songs, follow the church program but I can feel the pain building. I run to the bathroom, avoiding the smiles of others as they pass me in the hall. I'm not ready for this to happen, but I don't think I can stop it. My heart pounds, I can't breathe.

Not here, not now. I'm not ready. It's crashing down on me. I tell myself I'll cry someday, when I have time, when I can let it wash me away and drown me, like a good flood.

Christine finds me. I put on that fake front of mine and we go home. I know one day I won't be able to stop it and it'll be a relief.

Don't Ask, Don't Tell

"How are you, *really?*" Someone asked me on the phone the other day, as if you can just unzip your soul and let it flop out on the table. I attempted to answer but she interrupted. She didn't *really* want to know.

Another friend of mine said that after her husband died, it felt as if her skin had been taken off, put back on inside out and that every one of her tiny nerve endings was dangling. Anything, any word, the slightest brush, sent her into agony. I feel so overwhelmed at the slightest thing. I'm raw.

There is a subtle art to being with people in times like these. We all tend to either avoid or fumble our words when we don't know exactly what to say, myself included. But there's something to be said for the quiet soul who sits beside you, and says nothing.

Boundaries

Mother was some kind of boundary or anchor that I built my daily routine around. Now that she's gone, I'm floundering. Everything seems so big and overwhelming. There are so many choices, and I'm expected to do so much. I realize I'm the one putting expectations on myself, but they're still there, no matter who's imposing them. I feel like I'm supposed to do something now, or be something that she was somehow keeping me from.

I've been in no man's land, unconnected with the living, unconnected with the dead, unable to reach over and grab hold of the life I once had, or that other life that is to come.

A Good Losing

I'm ready. I've signed up for Weight Watchers. I need to turn back the last three or four years of my life and recapture my youth. Not in a teenagey, let's-go-party way, but to recapture my joy. I don't need to get old yet. I need to lose twenty-five pounds. I can hardly say it: twenty-five pounds. I've been denying it for so long. I bought into that whole "You're forty, it's inevitable" line. Well, it's not.

I signed up for Weight Watchers, threw away any temptations from the pantry and refrigerator and got on the treadmill. I need to consume myself in something big. School doesn't start back for a few weeks and I have all this pent-up energy. But it's deeper than feeling antsy or losing weight, it's about becoming this new person.

Madeleine L'Engle said, "*The great part about growing older is that you get to keep all the other ages you've ever been.*" I get to keep being a wife and mother, and being my mother's daughter and my Daddy's little girl. I get to keep it all, and I get to see what else is out there.

Pretending

I'm surprised at some people's candor in jumping right in and asking me about those final days and hours.

"Did she talk any? What was it like?" my mother-in-law asked.

That's better than the whole avoidance game. It's odd to think that we all must die but know so little about it. We all have loved ones—mothers, fathers, grandmothers, aunts, cousins, friends—who die over the course of our lifetime, and still we hesitate even to mention death. Maybe we have to block death out in order to stay alive. We have to pretend it's not there. It remains mysterious and incomprehensible. Maybe we're just not meant to wrap our arms, our minds, or our souls around such a formidable foe.

When I Miss Her

I miss Mother when I go to the grocery store. Since I'm no longer eligible to park in the parking spaces for the handicapped, I must walk by the light blue and white lines as I head across the parking lot that no longer takes me ten minutes to cross. I see Mother grip the handle of the grocery cart and remember the freedom this rolling walker gave her. I still see her curved spine dipping, her stockings slowly sagging from above her knees and eventually bunching around her ankles. I see her silhouette, complete with a bright blue nylon cap and its hundreds of petal-shaped pieces that made her head look like a massive flower. Some people loved her hat, others made fun of it, snickered about it behind our backs, but there were a few who found her and her blue hat endearing.

I miss her as I pass by the bananas. She said they gave her potassium and ate one a day. I had to buy seven a week—not six, not eight—though I often cheated, hoping to tide her over a day or two. Sometimes I get the urge to eat one in case I, too, am low on potassium. Any fruit she ate had to be peeled, cored and washed until it practically no longer resembled anything that ever lived. Apples were pale and tinged brown, grapes looked naked and embarrassed without their skins.

I miss her when I pass the Little Debbie display. Her face would light up at the sound of me opening the cellophane wrapper of an oatmeal pie.

I miss not picking up her half gallon of milk, her apple juice and her frozen dinners. I knew which ones she liked—the meatloaf, beef tips and flounder, nothing with pasta, very little chicken. Ice-cream bars remind me of her dying, not living. I can't bring myself to eat one, or even buy them anymore.

I miss her small talk with the cashier, the slightly condescending way she treated the help, and the times she surprised me with genuine kindness and humor. As time went on, she took forever to get out her wallet, and two forevers to pull out her credit cards. She could no longer differentiate a Visa card from a debit card, from a license. She'd just let them pick, holding the plastic squares out innocently like a hand of playing cards. I always tried to catch her before she let strangers rifle through her entire wallet and checkbook. By then, some of her prejudices had diminished and she chitchatted with anyone who caught her eye, regardless of race, which was a pleasant change, though unreliable. She insisted the baggers carry our groceries to the car, no matter how few we had, and she saw no need to tip them. I'd slip them a dollar or two after buckling her in. Tipping never was her thing.

Now I just go to the store like anyone else. No one to slow me down, no one to check on, no bananas to count, no Little Debbies to hide so she won't eat them all in two days. It's just ordinary, and what once seemed a bother, is now missed.

The Color of Youth

Christine has moved into Mother's apartment. She has painted a poppy-orange accent wall in the living room and the others a buttery yellow. There's a black futon, an entertainment center, a new ceiling fan and French doors off the living room. Black, square Japanese-style dishes line the white shelves along with fat wine goblets, set in perfect order. A screen covered with decorative scarves and bodices divides the room.

Mother's bedroom, once stark white, is now Mediterranean blue with white trim, There are white louvered closet doors and a large, Asian paper globe hanging from the ceiling that emits a warm moon-glow over my daughter's white down-covered bed. The apartment smells of jasmine, and the entire place whispers the promise of a young life.

I can go back there now and have only a wisp of those last few weeks. I sit on the edge of Christine's bed and play with Kismet, our Alaskan Malamute, and though I can't completely relax, I'm better. Mother's belongings are scattered around my home, on shelves, in crammed-full closets, in Rubbermaid containers, and under beds. Each of the girls has pieces of Mother's furniture, artwork, and pictures of Nanny and Papa.

Yet Mother surprises us from time to time. Christine and I were looking for gift bags and found an embroidered Bible cover. She thought she might like it and reached for it. Inside was stuffed with all kinds of things that Mother must have put in there during her times of confusion when she was constantly packing purses and bags to go home. We found a shoe with a stocking stuffed inside it, a brooch, a letter opener, some hairpins, an old picture of her mother and a New Testament Bible. We stood in the hall and let the laughter and tears come

Mother's still with us; her antics are still surprising us. We put the Bible cover and all of its contents back inside the closet, hoping to keep her with us a little longer.

Garage Sale

Mother has taken over my house. She's oozing out of every closet and taking over with a vengeance. Books, scrapbooks, shoes, purses, pictures, knickknacks litter every corner of my home. I'm having a garage sale this weekend. Some of the extraneous, non-sentmental stuff taking up precious space has got to go.

Mother said if I ever tried to have a garage sale that she'd come back and haunt me. I'm willing to risk it at this point. If she does come and haunt, I'll charge for it. That ought to boost sales. Maybe the Egyptians had this problem and they came up with an ingenious solution. They convinced people, especially the kings and royalty, to be buried with their stuff. They told them they would need it in the afterlife. Smart.

Bitter-Sweet

I put Mother's wallet and glasses in the top drawer of my dresser today. They've been sitting on top of it since she died four months ago. Mother kept Daddy's wallet, pocketknife, comb, and a small Bible in a heart-shaped cedar box he gave her the second time they went on a date in 1925. Something about these wallets left intact creates a sort of bubble holding time and memory in perfect stillness. Their licenses, credit cards, photos and slips of paper remind me that they had everyday lives.

I place the cedar heart box containing Daddy's wallet on the living room coffee table along with three music boxes he gave to Mother while they were dating. I'll have to search for a box, some sort of keepsake, to store Mother's belongings in, but for now I need her to go in the drawer. I am finally able to enjoy placing "her" around my home. I can rest a glass clown on a table, a Dresden China piece on the sideboard, and stand back and appreciate it, though I'm still tender.

This makes me question this whole "here, not here" mindset we have. Giving a friend a bit of humorous advice prefaced with "as my Mama always said…" is a way of keeping her here. Will there always be a bitter side of sweet? Will death and dying burn away, so that I don't have to run straight into them before retrieving a remembrance?

I hear Mother all the time and quote her daily. My friend Debbie's teenage daughter asked her mother, "Don't you trust me?" The age-old question every parent is eventually asked, the question we all secretly know the answer to. My southern mother answered that question when I asked it two decades ago, " Honey, I don't trust *myself* in the dark."

Paper Trail

The death certificate came in the mail. It looks more formal, more legal than I expected. I open the long envelope and slide out the certificates, seven altogether. The funeral director asked me how many I wanted, and I asked him how many I should have. He said several so I just picked a number. The insurance companies want their own original copies, I need to take one to the bank, and I don't know what the others are for. I just got extras. They're on blue paper, eleven by fourteen, with that extra fourth fold. There's a border all the way around and at the top it says, *State of Florida*, then, *Office of Vital Statistics. Certified Copy*, then, *Certificate of Death, Florida*. So it's certified, Mother's dead.

They look so serious, more serious than Phillip's, or mine, or the girl's birth certificates; mine is on a five by seven sheet of paper. I guess going out is a bigger deal. I stare at the death certificate, remembering all the legal documents I've seen in my life—my birth certificate, the real one I didn't see until after I found my birth family; my adoptive birth certificate with my altered name; my marriage certificate, yet another name change. I stare at this legal paper as I did the others, with curiosity, as if I might read something, understand something about those I love, or even myself, as if a piece of paper could do that.

I scan the boxes—name, date of birth, birthplace, place of death: Hospital, Inpatient, ER/Outpatient, DOA, Nursing home, Residence, Other. Residence has an X in front of it. I keep scanning the page: Decedent's usual occupation: Minister. Kind of Business: Religion. Marital Status: Widowed.

I keep reading, read the funeral service licensee number and name, the doctor's name, the hour of death: 7:39 P.M. The cause of death: myocardial infarction. Heart attack. I wonder why they decided on that? I was the only one there. No one asked me.

I leave the certificates on the sideboard for a few days, picking them up now and then, reading a few more boxes, noticing my mother's mother's name, running my fingers over the raised seal and letting this sink in. I mail off the ones that need to be mailed, but leave a copy on the sideboard. It's several weeks before the papers stop pulling at my attention and I can put them away.

Thanksgiving Morning

I get out Mother's enamel fruit bowl, the one painted with apples and grapes and pineapples. I know it must be from the fifties. I get out the potatoes and peeler and begin scraping the brown strips that fly and stick to the edges of the bowl. The white chunks are placed in a Revere Ware boiler that Mother gave me as a wedding present twenty-three years ago. I fill it with cold water and a dash of salt, and as I turn on the burner I suddenly feel five again and can see the small mound of salt crystals in the center of Mother's palm and the quick turn of her wrist.

This is my first Thanksgiving without Mother here.

Sometimes she would stop right in the middle of her cooking, turn the pot upside down for inspection and lay it on the edge of the sink. She sprinkled it with salt and baking soda, then squeezed a little lemon juice from the yellow plastic lemon. Her fingers made little scrubbing circles with a sudsy Brillo pad, her shoulders hunched, her face intent and her whole body pressing down as if she could cleanse the world of its sin. I hung around to watch the quick rinse under the faucet. She tilted the pan for me to see the copper as it gleamed. Satisfied, I'd head outside to swing.

She's been gone five months now.

I watch and wait for the potatoes to boil, for the familiar starchy foam that gathers first around the edges, turning the water opaque as the potatoes dance. I carry the heavy pot to the sink. The kitchen window fogs from the hot air that rises as the potatoes hit the strainer. With a shake, I pour them back into the fruit bowl, and blend the soft squares with cream, salt, and butter. They give way with each press of the old masher, the red stripe of paint flaking on the handle.

I spoon the fluffy potatoes into the green flute-edged bowl then remember, this bowl was used for the Waldorf salad, not the potatoes. I'm too tired to find another bowl, so I take them to the table, already set with my mother's grandmother's crocheted tablecloth and tell myself, no one will notice. Besides, does anyone but me like apples, walnuts, mayonnaise and raisins anyway?

With a snap of the Tupperware lid, I place a dozen cold deviled eggs into the heavy divided egg plate. I see Mother's hand take two, three, four, then another after a slice of both the pumpkin and pecan pie. Aromas of turkey and pole beans fill the air. I cut up bacon to flavor the beans and watch them simmer with crescents of translucent onion. Mother liked her vegetables tender—they tasted like mush to me; for Thanksgiving, I cook them a little longer.

I would stop and cry, but it would take too long, and the rolls would burn.

The buns, too hot to simply pick up, get shoved or tossed from the aluminum foil-covered cookie sheet into the silver bread warmer, the round one with penguins carved on the sides. I wonder, how many dinners of my childhood did I spend staring at those flightless birds? Each year, my head slightly higher, I viewed life from a different perspective. I can't find the top of the warmer, it probably got lost in the move, so I fold a napkin over the rolls to keep them warm.

I put out the turkey on its tray and set it in the middle of the table. I get out a pale yellow organza apron, stiff with starch. Mother must have ironed it some ten, maybe twenty years ago, and although it's a bit musty and dinner is ready, I tie it around my waist. I remember the slam then the slide of the iron, and that sweet, hot steamy fragrance of starch on cotton. I used to watch Mother take the tip of the silver triangle and go around tiny buttons, pressing Daddy's white Sunday collars. A strand of her hair slipped across her forehead as she warned me to step back. I brought my crayons and paper and drew at the old-fashioned school desk she put in the kitchen and that Daddy had painted gold. They loved gold. I liked hearing the *phish* sound the iron made after each burst of steam, as if exhausted from its labor.

I call everyone to the table and pull out a chair, the chair Mother sat in last Thanksgiving, and sit down.

I pour red wine into crystal goblets, given to Mother by her sister-in-law for a wedding gift some sixty-seven years ago. Mother never used them, but I've already broken one. We fill plates and my husband, our daughters and our guests all take hands, and we bow our heads in thanks.

I never knew I'd miss her so much.

A Hatful of Recollections

Mother used to get up with me when I was in elementary school. She fixed breakfast, eggs and bacon, whether I wanted it or not. Then she'd pray with me before I left for school. We stood at the threshold of the door, paused. I closed my eyes, shifted my heavy book bag, wriggled into my coat and waited for Daddy to drive me to school. They were both retired and they centered their lives around mine—a bad scenario for an only child who craved attention the way Southerners crave sweet tea.

Later, during high school, when the thrill of motherhood had waned, Mother relied on me to get my own breakfast. Not that I wanted any, ever, but she wouldn't let up. I pressed the toaster lever down, so if she checked, it would still be warm. I stuck my hand in the bread wrapper and sprinkled a few crumbs on the counter, ran the knife across the butter, sometimes dipping a spoon in the pear preserves, all an elaborate hoax in order not to do what she wanted.

She stumbled out, in her nylon gown, her teased bouffant deflated from a restless night on the satin pillowcase. She prayed. I waited, shifting my book bag and wriggling into my coat. She made me put on a sock cap in the winter, relying on the medical advice that seventy percent of the body's heat is lost off the top of your head. I stood across the street and waited for the bus. As soon as it pulled up and blocked her view, I whipped the cap off, boarded the bus and put on my makeup—something else she didn't allow.

Why I felt so compelled not to do whatever she insisted on is a part of the mother-daughter dance. I had to defy her, I knew no other way. I yanked off that hat and everything she told me. Now my own children half-heartedly tolerate my advice. I don't insist on the hats but other things are non-negotiable, like curfews and calling me when they're out. I feel their resistance and take it in stride.

At forty-one, I eat breakfast every morning. I never miss. Sometimes I even wear a cap when it's cold.

Quite a Pair

I've come to realize something I would have vehemently denied up until now. Mother and I were suited for each other. If anyone had said that but me, I would have been insulted. Mother had qualities I'd like not to claim. I have a few of my own I'd like not to claim. I'm just coming to accept my life—not as some pansy story. It wasn't all wonderful, but now, I'm not in so many knots. I can look at it all with some kind of perspective.

Both of us are outgoing, neither one prone to depression, both emotional, she more than I, I'd like to think. (I am aware of the tense issue: I am present, she is past. This great divide wreaks havoc with our language and even more havoc with my heart.)

Who else could have ridden the swells of Mother's temper? Who else could have been stubborn enough to spread crumbs on the counter and yank sock caps off? Who else would walk down that last dark hall but someone who so needed a family that keeping one together meant everything?

Guilt/No Guilt

I went for a bike ride the other day and spoke to a neighbor who didn't know that my mother had passed away. This neighbor is a nurse and for some reason I'm not sure of now, I told her how I had managed to keep Mother at home and fulfill her wish not to go into a nursing home. I wasn't really enjoying this conversation. I'm cautious about where and when and to whom I talk about my mother. It's still painful, especially the part about her last few months. I used to wonder why people who had recently lost loved ones didn't talk about them more. Now I know why. It's not because they're not thinking about them. It's because words don't soothe the way memories do.

We kept talking, though I wanted to change the subject to something mundane, like lawn fertilizers, or our lackadaisical mail carrier who seems to prefer to actually hit the mailbox post, forcing the door to open on impact. But my neighbor, a nurse with enough formal training to bug the everlasting fool out of you in times of deep pain, wouldn't let the subject rest.

"The good part is that you kept her home and so you have no guilt," she said.

I almost fell off my bike—how had she come through fifty-something years of life and relationships—I don't care if it was just a series of pets— without experiencing any guilt?

"Of course I have guilt! I don't think you can have any sort of real relationship that doesn't involve a certain amount of guilt." She looked at me from beneath her blonde bob and I believed I had undone something.

I've decided to bike the other way for a while. I'm feeling too guilty about bursting her bubble that life has no guilt to ride past her house anytime soon. She may be inside sitting in her recliner, all but comatose, her top lip quivering, her head filling with fifty-years of repressed regrets, and I wouldn't want to feel responsible for that.

Measuring Goodness

Elizabeth Smart was found yesterday. She's a little girl who was abducted from her home in Utah. CNN covered her return extensively. They keep using the word miracle. A miracle links us directly to God, bypassing logic and physical law on its way. It tells us we're not in charge and there are happenings beyond us and our doings. Everyone's talking about Elizabeth. The whole country is rejoicing, reminding me of the words from the Bible in the story of the Prodigal Son, "...*once was lost, now is found.*"

I wonder if Mother had anything to do with this miracle? I know that sounds absurd, Mother's been gone since July, almost nine months now. But a few years ago, when Mother was in her late eighties and still living at home, I was emptying her garbage one day and grabbed a plastic grocery bag full of papers. When I looked inside, I saw hundreds of those postcard mail-outs we all receive that advertise something or other and have a small picture of a missing person in the corner. They read, "Have you seen me?"

I wondered why she collected these. I thought I was used to her bizarre hoarding habits. This one had me stumped.

"Those aren't trash." She reached for the bag.

"You don't need them." I held on.

"Those are all the missing children. I pray for them every day," she said, looking shy as if I had caught her at something. She took the bag from my hands.

She had no idea what her wide-spanned mood swings did to a child or a relationship. But in this one gesture, this private compassion for these missing children, she had wiped a multitude of sins from the ledger of her soul.

Do we even have this whole good/bad thing down right? We think the Bible has only one interpretation, which Jesus tried to shed some light on, but most of us trudge up the hill to Mount Sinai and the stone Ten Commandments instead of running to Golgotha and clinging to the cross. We rationalize that if we keep those ten rules, we will be rewarded with the opening of the pearly gates. But what if God has a different measuring stick? What if, even though we've done a whole lot of wrongs, something miraculous can take place? In one moment, and with one choice, what if we erase all that we've done, and in that brief instant, God sees straight to the good and the holy within us?

Mother would have turned ninety-three this month. It will be the first birthday without her, another day in a long line of firsts I'm dreading. The world has had fewer prayers these past nine months, though I wonder if Mother's been pulling strings from the other side. And now I'm wondering if maybe it's time I take up the slack.

Headstones

I haven't cried all that much about Mother's death. I'm strange like that. I'll well up during a Hallmark commercial and then sit stone dry at a funeral. But today, eleven months since my mother's death, I've finally gotten around to ordering her headstone and I know that I can no longer avoid the tears. I don't know why I've procrastinated about either for so long. Maybe it was my last attempt to keep it from not being real. I guess I thought that if I could avoid seeing Mother's name carved in stone then it wouldn't be final. I take a deep breath and call the cemetery to place the order.

"Now, how do you want it to read, hon?" the man asks in his gravelly Georgia way.

"You may have to help me," I stammer, caught off guard.

I haven't thought this through. Should I hang up? I don't know what I want on Mother's headstone. I tell him who I am, where Mother's plot is. He knows. He says he's been waiting on the DeVault family for forty years now.

"I want it to look like Daddy's," is all I can think to say. "In loving memory," I go on, seeing hundreds of headstones in my mind, remembering all the times I played as a child at Greenwood Cemetery, romping around the markers.

Mother and Daddy took me to the funerals of all their friends and family members, and I wasn't the only child on those rolling hills where blinding white marble blocks gleamed in the sun. I liked the Jewish section because they put pictures on their headstones and placed little rocks around the graves.

"In loving memory—" the man interrupts my thoughts, repeating my words.

Loving memory suddenly has meaning. I've read these words countless times. Tears surface. I imagine what it will look like.

"In Loving Memory. Noveline DeVault, March 21, 1911… wait, that's not right. I mean, March 22. That's her birthday."

"When did she die, hon?" His question throws me.

"I don't know." I feel lost. "I'll go get the death certificate." Like an obedient child I run to find it. "June 21, 2002," I read.

"Can we add wife and mother?" I ask. Tears are gathering in the holes of the phone. I'm losing my voice. I don't want to have to sniff. *Oh God, I can't hold it back.*

"Sure. We'll take a picture and send it to you as soon as we get it in."

I recite the credit card numbers, trying to say each one distinctly through my sobs. There's no holding it back now.

My mother is gone. I've ordered her headstone, so I guess that makes it real.

Here

Almost a year has passed. I walk to the kitchen. I see Mother again, clear in my mind. I don't have to run this time.

She's holding onto my counter and eating the cookies. I pretend not to notice.

"What have you got to drink?" she asks.

"Milk."

"No."

"Apple juice."

"No."

"Sprite?"

"No." I'm getting aggravated. "Lately, Sprite's been tasting like cat pee." I laugh. She laughs.

"Coke—how about some Coke?"

"Coca-cola sounds good."

I pull out a chair and help her sit down, then pour her a glass and take it to her—one ice-cube and a straw, just the way she likes. She drinks it; each gulp is hard. She makes a face like a little kid eating something sour. Her eyes tear up.

"Give me some more."

I pour more and have some myself.

Good times surface. I've lost twenty-five pounds. I'm doing well in school. The girls are living, really living. I'm keeping my word. I'm not as manic as I was. I don't have as many nightmares and I don't have to take anything to sleep. I stay home more, because I don't have to run. We're planning our twenty-fifth anniversary for next September.

There's not a day that Mother's not here, but it's a good here.

Rain and Wine

It's my birth month. I need something big. This spring has been filled with Mother's void. Her birthday, my birthday, and soon, the anniversary of her passing all lined up, waiting for me to feel each of them. I barely seem to get over one before the next one nudges into place. This time last year was so heavy that I've determined that this month of May will be overflowing with long beach walks and midnight stargazing. I plan to eat dark cherries, read fat novels and grab life every chance I get.

I've ordered four tickets to see James Taylor, and Phillip and I plan to invite our friends, Debbie and her husband Danté, to the concert. Not since I turned sixteen and Phillip gave me my first album has James not been in my house, my car and in my head. I truly believe that people come in keys. Some are B flats, others A minors. We either harmonize with another person or create a dissonance so profound we walk away not quite knowing why. James strikes a soul chord in me like the pull of the bow across the strings of a cello. I met him once. He was wonderful.

We pile into the car, excited as teens. I wear my favorite sundress and dangly earrings. We put on *How Sweet It Is*, and all of us sing out the open car windows. We park and head down to the pavilion. It's outdoor seating on a May Sunday. Hundreds stand in line with lawn chairs and blankets. There's a look people get when they're expecting something good to happen. They're alert, at ease, and yet anxious all at the same time. I see that look all around me; no doubt I have it as well. We're antsy; smiles sneak out around the corners of mouths and the little lines around the eyes give away a kid-like joy.

Plump rain clouds slide into place overhead just as the band comes to the stage, but everyone ignores the threat and cheers like crazy. James, with his lanky arms and legs and humble smile comes to the microphone. He gives the audience a small bow. The audience whistles, claps, and screams. James turns to his band, and I can see a ripple of recognition as each member takes his place and the music begins.

"*Whenever I see your smiling face…*" James's voice fills my head.

It starts to sprinkle. Phillip's gone to get drinks I stand, kick off my shoes and sway, arms lifted as in church. The sprinkling becomes a downpour. I laugh, turn to Debbie and we shake our wet hair, laughing at how crazy it all is. My dress is sticking to my bra and the top of my thighs. I realize I'm not wearing a slip, consider sitting down, thinking for one moment of my mother. I stay standing and smile.

I look for Phillip, but can't see him past the crowd. Music saturates the air, and I can feel the pulse of the bass. I sit, give myself a minute to relax, cross my feet and watch the water trail off my ankles. The rain is steady and warm. I turn to Debbie and Danté; our clothes are plastered to our skin, our hair heavy with rain. We laugh—we might as well. Other people pull out yellow ponchos. We don't have any. I don't want any.

It feels so good. I'm here, at a James Taylor concert in Florida. I live in Florida. James is playing *Shower the People*. I lick the rain off my lips. Debbie grabs my hand and gives it a squeeze.

Phillip comes back with a bucket of wine and four plastic glasses. He sits in a pool of water before I can wipe it off. It's doesn't matter, we're all drenched. He tries to tell me something, but the music is loud and wonderful. I take two glasses, and he holds two. He tries to open the wine—it's uncorked half way but won't come out. He holds the bottle up to his mouth and bites the cork out with his teeth. I nudge Debbie. We laugh at the cork between Phillip's teeth, his face wet and dripping. He's smiling. We each take a glass and toast as raindrops mingle with our wine.

We toast and laugh and sing.

Expecting

I've been hoping and even expecting the dolphins' return. This time last year, the torrential rains had finally ceased and the dolphins came out to play. I walk out to the edge of the river, listen for the *puh* of the blowhole, and scan the surface of the river, longing to see their familiar arc.

There it is! I let out a scream like I've never seen this before, turn, run to get my camera, then stop. I don't want to miss even one moment. The dolphins trace the shoreline, their sleek bodies catching the light. Sea gulls and egrets take off, and the dolphins submerge to their water-world. I stand still, content, expecting.

Bibliography

Albom, M. *Tuesdays With Morrie: An Old Man, A Young Man and Life's Greatest Lessons*. New York: Doubleday, 1997.

Davies, H.D., and M.P. Jensen. *Alzheimer's: The Answers You Need*. Forest Knolls, Calif.: Elder Books, 1998.

Davis, P. *The Long Goodbye: Memories of My Father*. New York: Penguin Group, 2005.

Didion, J. *The Year of Magical Thinking*. New York: Alfred A. Knopf, 2005.

Fox, M.J. *Lucky Man: A Memoir*. New York: Hyperion, 2002.

Kondracke, M. *Saving Millie: Life, Politics and Living with Parkinson's Disease*. New York: Ballantine, 2002.

Kushner, H.S. *When Bad Things Happen to Good People*. New York: Schocken, 1981.

L'Engle, M. *Summer of the Great Grandmother*. New York: Harper and Row, 1982.

Lewis, C.S. *A Grief Observed*. New York: Harper and Row, 1963.

Mace, N.L. and Rabins, P.V. *The 36-Hour Day: A Family Guide to Caring for Persons with Alzheimer Disease, Related Dementing Illnesses, and Memory Loss in Later Life*. Baltimore and London, The Johns Hopkins University Press, Third Edition, 1999.

Nuland, S. *How We Die: Reflections on Life's Final Chapter*. New York: Vintage, 1995.

Shaef, A.W. *Meditations for Women Who Do Too Much*. New York: Harper Collins, 1990.

Warner, M.A. *The Complete Guide to Alzheimer's Proofing Your Home*. West Lafayette, Ind.: Purdue University Press, 1998.

Zabbia, K.H. *Painted Diaries: A Mother and Daughter's Experience through Alzheimer's*. Minneapolis: Fairview Press, 1996.

For Children

Guthrie, D. *Grandpa Doesn't Know It's Me: A Family Adjusts to Alzheimer's Disease.* New York: Human Sciences Press, 1986.

Kroll, V. L. *Fireflies, Peach Pies, & Lullabies.* New York: Simon & Schuster, 1995

Williams, C.L. *If I Forget, You Remember.* New York: Delacorte Press, 1998.

Video

The Forgetting: A Portrait of Alzheimer's. Minneapolis: Twin Cities Publishing, Inc., PBS Program Club Pick, 2003.

APPENDIX

Many national organizations have local or state chapters. Check the Internet or your telephone directory.

Administration on Aging, 200 Independence Ave. S.W., Room 309, Washington, D.C. 20201; tel. 202-401-4541. Web site address: http://www.aoa.dhhs.gov. This organization can provide the address of the office on aging and nursing home ombudsperson nearest you.

Agency for Health Care Policy and Research, P.O. Box 8547, Silver Spring, Md. 20907-8547; tel. toll-free 800-358-9295. Web site address: http://www.ahcpr.gov. The AHCPR works to enhance the quality, appropriateness, and effectiveness of health care services and to improve access to care. It provides free publications about nursing home care.

Aging Network Services, 4400 East-West Highway, Suite 907, Bethesda, Md. 20814; tel. 301-657-4329. Web site address: http://www.agingnets.com. A nationwide network of private-practice geriatric social workers who serve as care managers for older parents who live at a distance.

Alliance of Information and Referral Systems, P.O. Box 31668, Seattle, Wash. 98103; tel. 206-632-2477. Web site address: http://www.airs.org. A professional organization that provides information and referrals in the human services.

Alzheimer's Association, 919 N. Michigan Ave., Suite 1000, Chicago, Ill. 60611-1676; tel. 800-272-3900. Web site address: http://www.alz.org. Call or write for information on services, programs, and publications or to find the chapter nearest you. The association has a lobbying branch: Public Policy Division, Alzheimer's Association, 1319 F St. N.W., Suite 710, Washington, D.C. 20004; tel. 202-393-7737.

Alzheimer's Disease Education and Referral Center, P.O. Box 8250, Silver Spring, Md. 20907-8250; tel. 301-495-3311/toll-free 800-438-4380. Web site address: http://www.alzheimers.org. A service of the National Institute on Aging, distributes information and free materials on a wide variety of topics related to Alzheimer's disease to health professionals, patients and their families, and the general public.

American Association of Homes and Services for the Aging, 901 E St. N.W., Suite 500, Washington, D.C. 20004; tel. 202-783-2242. Web site address: http://www.aahsa.org. Represents not-for-profit nursing homes, continuing-care retirement communities, senior housing facilities, assisted living facilities, and community services organizations dedicated to providing high-quality health care, housing, and services to the nation's elderly persons.

American Association of Retired Persons, 601 E St. N.W., Washington, D.C. 20049; tel. 202-434-2277/toll-free 800-424-3410. Web site address: http://www.aarp.org. A nonprofit, nonpartisan organization dedicated to helping older Americans achieve lives of independence, dignity, and purpose.

American Cancer Society, 1599 Clifton Rd. N.E., Atlanta, Ga. 30329; tel. 404-320-3333/toll-free 800-277-2345. Web site address: http://www.cancer.org.

American Diabetes Association, P.O. Box 25757, 1660 Duke St., Alexandria, Va. 22314; tel. 703-549-1500. Web site address: http://www.diabetes.org.

American Geriatrics Society, 770 Lexington Ave., Suite 300, New York, N.Y. 10021; tel. 212-308-1414/toll-free 800-247-4779. Web site address: http://www. americangeriatrics.org. A professional association of geriatric physicians.

American Heart Association, 7272 Greenville Ave., Dallas, Tex. 75231; tel. 214-373-6300. Web site address: http://www.americanheart.org.

American Society on Aging, 833 Market St., Suite 511, San Francisco, Calif. 94103; tel. 415-974-9600/toll-free 800-537-9728. Web site address: http://www.asaging. org. Publishes the journal *Generations* and the newsletter *Aging Today*.

Children of Aging Parents, 1609 Woodbourne Rd., Suite 302-A, Levittown, Pa. 19057; tel. 215-945-6900/toll-free 800-227-7294. Web site address: http://www. careguide.net. Provides information and referrals for caregivers of older people.

National Adult Day Services Association, 409 3rd St. S.W., Suite 200, Washington, D.C. 20024; tel. 202-479-6682. Web site address: http://www.ncoa.org/nadsa/.

National Association for Homecare, 228 7th St. S.E., Washington, D.C. 20003; tel. 202-547-4724. Web site address: http://www.nahc.org. A trade association representing home care providers.

National Association of Social Workers, 750 1st St. N.E., Suite 700, Washington, D.C. 20002; tel. 202-408-8600/toll-free 800-638-8799. Web site address: http:// www.socialworkers.org.

National Citizens' Coalition for Nursing Home Reform, 1424 16th St. N.W., Suite 202, Washington, D.C. 20036; tel. 202-332-2275. Web site address: http://www. nccnhr.org. A national nonprofit organization concerned with improving the long-term care system and the quality of life for long-term care residents.

National Council on the Aging, 409 3rd St. S.W., Suite 200, Washington, D.C. 20024; tel. 202-479-1200/toll-free 800-424-9046. Web site address: http://www. ncoa.org. Publishes an annotated bibliography; has information about adult day care, home care, and other respite care.

National Family Caregiver Association, 10605 Concord St., Suite 501, Kensington, Md. 20895-2504; tel. 301-942-6430/toll-free 800-896-3650. Web site address: http://www.nfcacares.org.

National Hospice Organization, 1901 N. Moore St., Suite 901, Arlington, Va. 22209; tel. 703-243-5900/toll-free 800-658-8898. Web site address: http://www. nho.org.

National Mental Health Association, 1021 Prince St., Alexandria, Va. 22314; tel. 703-684-7722/toll-free 800-969-6642. Web site address: http://www.nmha.org.

National Stroke Association, 96 Inverness Dr. East, Suite I, Englewood, Colo. 80112-5112; tel. 303-649-9299/toll-free 800-787-6537. Web site address: http://www. stroke.org.

Safe Return, P.O. Box 9307, St. Louis, Mo. 63117-0307; toll-free tel. 888-572-8566. A joint program of the Alzheimer's Association and the National Center for Missing Persons. Caregivers fit a person who has dementia with a bracelet showing the person's name, the registered caregiver's name, and Safe Return's toll-free number (800-572-1122) to aid in that person's return should he or she become disoriented or lost.

U.S. Department of Veterans Affairs, 1120 Vermont Ave. N.W., Washington, D.C. 20421; toll-free tel. 800-827-1000.

FEDERAL INSTITUTES
National Institute of Mental Health, Adult and Geriatric Treatment and Preventive Interventions Research Branch, Room 10-75, 5600 Fishers Lane, Rockville, Md. 20857; tel. 301-443-1185.

National Institute of Neurological Disorders and Stroke, Office of Scientific and Health Reports, National Institutes of Health, Building 31, Room 8A-06, 31 Center Dr., MSC 2540, Bethesda, Md. 20892-2540; tel. 301-496-5751/toll-free 800-352-9424. Web site address: http://www.ninds.nih.gov.

National Institute on Aging, National Institutes of Health, 31 Center Dr., Building 31, Room 5C27, Bethesda, Md. 20892-2292; tel. 301-496-1752/toll-free 800-438-4380. Distributes brochures and information about the federally funded dementia centers and other federal initiatives; publishes a free directory of organizations that serve elderly people.

INTERNATIONAL AGENCIES

Alzheimer Europe, 145 Route de Thionville, L-2611 Luxembourg; tel. 352 29.79.70, fax 352 29.79.72. Web site address: http://www.alzheimer-europe. org. An organization dedicated to raising awareness about all forms of dementia through coordination and cooperation among Alzheimer organizations throughout Europe.

Alzheimer's Disease International, 45/46 Lower Marsh, London SE1 7RG, United Kingdom; tel. 44 171 620-3011, fax 44 171 401-7351. Web site address: http:// www.alzdisint.demon.co.uk. An international organization of associations dedicated to dementia.

INTERNET SITES

AgeNet. Web site address: http://www.agenet.com. Also http://www.caregivers. com. An information and referral network designed to communicate information about products and services that are important to enhancing the quality of life of older adults and their families.

Alzheimer's Association. Web site address: http://www.alz.org. Especially for: Living with Alzheimer's, Caregivers, Health Professionals and Quality Care.

National Family Caregivers Association. Web site address: http://nfcacares.org

National Institute on Aging. Web site address: http://www.nia.nih.gov/ Alzheimers//Alzheimer's Disease Education and Referral Center.

National Parkinson's Foundation. Web site address: http://www.parkinson.org. A national organization dedicated to the research, care, and hope worldwide.

Parkinson's Disease Foundation. Web site address:http://www.pdf.org. Supporting the highest quality research in the cause and cure of Parkinson's.

SeniorNet. Web site address: http://www.seruornet.org. A national nonprofit organization whose mission is to build a community of computer-using seniors.

Index

About the author

"I was adopted at age four to Southern, fundamentalist parents in their mid-fifties—what more could a writer want?"

Carol D. O'Dell's world changed the day she was adopted. She knew she had to preserve her spirit and the memory of the family she left behind. Taken from Florida to Atlanta and raised by adoring parents of a fiery faith, Carol was steeped in Bible stories and bedtime stories. She is drawn to the Southern, the reverent and irreverent found in art, nature, faith, and man. Her stories have been described as "full of magic and wonder" and "moments of offered grace." MOTHERING MOTHER tells the story of a daughter's devotion and a family's promise.

Carol D. O'Dell's short stories, essays and excerpts have appeared in numerous publications including AIM Magazine, Atlanta Magazine and MARGIN. She participated in the 2005 Summer Literary Series in St. Petersburg, Russia, and is a John Woods Scholarship recipient for the 2007 Prague Summer Program. She teaches creative writing at community centers, schools, libraries and the Florida Governor's Honor's Program. She is also an inspirational speaker on writing, caregiving and adoption issues. Her website is www.caroldodell.com <http://www.caroldodell.com/>

Provocative. Bold. Controversial.

The Game
A thriller by Derek Armstrong

Reality television becomes too real when a killer stalks the cast on America's number one live-broadcast reality show.
■ "A series to watch ... Armstrong injects the trope with new vigor." *Booklist*
US$ 24.95 | Pages 352, cloth hardcover
ISBN 978-1-60164-001-7 | EAN: 9781601640017
LCCN 2006930183

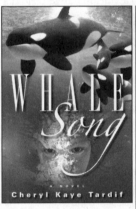

Rabid
A novel by T K Kenyon

A sexy, savvy, darkly funny tale of ambition, scandal, forbidden love and murder. Nothing is sacred. The graduate student, her professor, his wife, her priest: four brilliantly realized characters spin out of control in a world where science and religion are in constant conflict.
■ "Kenyon is definitely a keeper." STARRED REVIEW, *Booklist*
US$ 26.95
Pages 480, cloth hardcover
ISBN 978-1-60164-002-4
EAN 9781601640024
LCCN 2006930189

Whale Song
A novel by Cheryl Kaye Tardif

Whale Song is a haunting tale of change and choice. Cheryl Kaye Tardif's beloved novel—a "wonderful novel that will make a wonderful movie" according to *Writer's Digest*—asks the difficult question, which is the higher morality, love or law?
■ "Crowd-pleasing ... a big hit." *Booklist*
US$ 12.95
Pages 208, UNA trade paper
ISBN 978-1-60164-007-9
EAN 9781601640079
LCCN 2006930188

Shadow of Innocence
A mystery by Ric Wasley

The Thin Man meets *Pulp Fiction* in a unique mystery set amid the drugs-and-music scene of the sixties that touches on all our societal taboos. *Shadow of Innocence* has it all: adventure, sleuthing, drugs, sex, music and a perverse shadowy secret that threatens to tear apart a posh New England town.
US$ 24.95
Pages 304, cloth hardcover
ISBN 978-1-60164-006-2
EAN 9781601640062
LCCN 2006930187